S. Hrg. 114–408

HOW THE INTERNET OF THINGS CAN BRING U.S. TRANSPORTATION AND INFRASTRUCTURE INTO THE 21ST CENTURY

HEARING

BEFORE THE

SUBCOMMITTEE ON SURFACE TRANSPORTATION AND MERCHANT MARINE INFRASTRUCTURE, SAFETY AND SECURITY

OF THE

COMMITTEE ON COMMERCE, SCIENCE, AND TRANSPORTATION UNITED STATES SENATE

ONE HUNDRED FOURTEENTH CONGRESS

SECOND SESSION

JUNE 28, 2016

Printed for the use of the Committee on Commerce, Science, and Transportation

U.S. GOVERNMENT PUBLISHING OFFICE

22–359 PDF   WASHINGTON : 2016

For sale by the Superintendent of Documents, U.S. Government Publishing Office
Internet: bookstore.gpo.gov   Phone: toll free (866) 512–1800; DC area (202) 512–1800
Fax: (202) 512–2104   Mail: Stop IDCC, Washington, DC 20402–0001

SENATE COMMITTEE ON COMMERCE, SCIENCE, AND TRANSPORTATION

ONE HUNDRED FOURTEENTH CONGRESS

SECOND SESSION

JOHN THUNE, South Dakota, *Chairman*

ROGER F. WICKER, Mississippi
ROY BLUNT, Missouri
MARCO RUBIO, Florida
KELLY AYOTTE, New Hampshire
TED CRUZ, Texas
DEB FISCHER, Nebraska
JERRY MORAN, Kansas
DAN SULLIVAN, Alaska
RON JOHNSON, Wisconsin
DEAN HELLER, Nevada
CORY GARDNER, Colorado
STEVE DAINES, Montana

BILL NELSON, Florida, *Ranking*
MARIA CANTWELL, Washington
CLAIRE McCASKILL, Missouri
AMY KLOBUCHAR, Minnesota
RICHARD BLUMENTHAL, Connecticut
BRIAN SCHATZ, Hawaii
EDWARD MARKEY, Massachusetts
CORY BOOKER, New Jersey
TOM UDALL, New Mexico
JOE MANCHIN III, West Virginia
GARY PETERS, Michigan

NICK ROSSI, *Staff Director*
ADRIAN ARNAKIS, *Deputy Staff Director*
REBECCA SEIDEL, *General Counsel*
JASON VAN BEEK, *Deputy General Counsel*
KIM LIPSKY, *Democratic Staff Director*
CHRIS DAY, *Democratic Deputy Staff Director*
CLINT ODOM, *Democratic General Counsel and Policy Director*

———

SUBCOMMITTEE ON SURFACE TRANSPORTATION AND MERCHANT MARINE INFRASTRUCTURE, SAFETY AND SECURITY

DEB FISCHER, Nebraska, *Chairman*
ROGER F. WICKER, Mississippi
ROY BLUNT, Missouri
KELLY AYOTTE, New Hampshire
JERRY MORAN, Kansas
DAN SULLIVAN, Alaska
RON JOHNSON, Wisconsin
DEAN HELLER, Nevada
STEVE DAINES, Montana

CORY BOOKER, New Jersey, *Ranking*
MARIA CANTWELL, Washington
CLAIRE McCASKILL, Missouri
AMY KLOBUCHAR, Minnesota
RICHARD BLUMENTHAL, Connecticut
BRIAN SCHATZ, Hawaii
EDWARD MARKEY, Massachusetts
TOM UDALL, New Mexico

CONTENTS

HOW THE INTERNET OF THINGS CAN BRING U.S. TRANSPORTATION AND INFRASTRUCTURE INTO THE 21ST CENTURY

TUESDAY, JUNE 28, 2016

U.S. SENATE,
SUBCOMMITTEE ON SURFACE TRANSPORTATION AND
MERCHANT MARINE INFRASTRUCTURE, SAFETY AND SECURITY,
COMMITTEE ON COMMERCE, SCIENCE, AND TRANSPORTATION,
Washington, DC.

The Subcommittee met, pursuant to notice, at 9:45 a.m. in room SR–253, Russell Senate Office Building, Hon. Deb Fischer, Chairman of the Subcommittee, presiding.

Present: Senators Fischer [presiding], Ayotte, Heller, Daines, Johnson, Booker, Cantwell, Klobuchar, Markey, and Blumenthal.

OPENING STATEMENT OF HON. DEB FISCHER, U.S. SENATOR FROM NEBRASKA

Senator FISCHER. Good morning. I am pleased to convene the Senate Subcommittee on Surface Transportation and Merchant Marine Infrastructure, Safety and Security for today's hearing entitled, "How the Internet of Things Can Bring U.S. Transportation and Infrastructure into the 21st Century." This hearing will examine how the Internet of Things can advance our Nation's transportation and infrastructure system.

America's transportation network is well-positioned to benefit from new developments in technology. For example, the Internet of Things offers new ways to help alleviate congestion on our Nation's roads, reduce cargo shipping delays at ports, and monitor rail and pipeline infrastructure safety. This growing interconnected network can inform policymakers on where to invest limited resources in road and bridge maintenance.

In March, Senator Booker and I joined Senators Ayotte and Schatz to introduce the Developing Innovation and Growing the Internet of Things Act, or the DIGIT Act. This bipartisan legislation builds on our resolution, which passed the Senate last year. It calls for a nationwide strategy to drive development of the Internet of Things.

The DIGIT Act would convene a working group of private and public sector stakeholders to offer recommendations to Congress. They would focus on how to plan for and encourage the growth of the Internet of Things. Our bill would begin discussions on the future of this network, and ensure that the United States is adopting policies that accelerate innovation and allow it to thrive.

This could have a positive effect on transportation. For instance, global supply chains represent a major opportunity to take advantage of the Internet of Things to grow exports and imports. In today's just-in-time shipping environment, time is money and efficiency is key.

According to the U.S. Department of Transportation, by 2045, freight volumes will increase by 45 percent. DOT in its Beyond Traffic report found that transportation delays have a high cost. For example, Nike spends an additional $4 million per week in extra inventory to compensate for shipping delays. The same report found that a week-long disruption at our Nation's two largest ports, LA and Long Beach, would cost our economy as much as $150 million per day.

Meanwhile, supply chains are changing rapidly in response to transportation delays and alternative options. For example, after 9 years, the $5.4 billion Panama Canal expansion is expected to open this week. Following the project's completion, the Panama Canal will be able to process ships nearly 3 times as large as before and will provide a greater connection between our East Coast ports and Asian export markets.

A recent white paper co-authored by C.H. Robinson and the Boston Consulting Group pointed out that the canal's expansion promises to reorient the landscape of the logistics industry and alter the decisionmaking calculus of shippers that the canal serves.

Delays in our logistics chain raise costs for shippers, infrastructure operators, carriers, and, yes, consumers. By increasing connectivity and real-time data flows between stakeholders, our transportation network and its users will gain productivity.

Infrastructure design, construction, maintenance, and safety will also benefit from improved data and connectivity.

State and local highway officials constantly face challenges when allocating limited resources to an array of transportation projects. For example, AECOM has established a Self-Monitoring Analysis and Reporting Technology system, known as SMART, to remotely monitor bridges, dams, and other transportation assets. AECOM's SMART infrastructure seeks to use the Internet of Things to enhance the operating efficiencies of infrastructure and lengthen the life of these critical assets.

Real-time monitoring represents a critical analytic tool that can enable States and localities to expend highway dollars in a risk-based manner, thereby bolstering safety and infrastructure reliability.

As part of the FAST Act, I worked with my colleagues on this committee to author a robust national freight policy that will provide States with greater resources to designate critical urban and rural corridors. Congress also expanded the objectives of the Intelligent Transportation System program, which seeks to integrate technology, communications, and data into our transportation network to include enhancing our national freight network.

Senator Booker and I have been working together to better understand the possibilities of the Internet of Things and to educate our Senate colleagues on them.

I'm pleased that we have an exceptional group of stakeholders appearing before the Subcommittee today. We are fortunate to have officials who are developing policy at the Federal and local levels, and I am eager to hear how private sector stakeholders are utilizing the Internet, data, and technology to manage infrastructure projects and advance freight and passenger transportation networks.

I would now like to invite my friend, Senator Cory Booker, our Ranking Member, for any comments he may have.

STATEMENT OF HON. CORY BOOKER, U.S. SENATOR FROM NEW JERSEY

Senator BOOKER. Thank you very much, Chairwoman Fischer.

I, first of all, want to submit my formal opening remarks to the record. I am kind of geeking out about this meeting, and I think this is tremendous that you all are here.

There is a lot going on in Washington today, some of it laced with lots of partisanship, but this hearing right now with my partner on a lot of things, more than I could've imagined, the Chairwoman and I have found a lot of things to work on that are really forward-facing, trying to make not only government more efficient and effective, but really trying to echo what was bipartisan work of the past.

It was a great Republican President named Eisenhower who understood, to help the private sector flourish, there has to be creative public-private partnerships. One of the great ways to create connectivity of the past was just building roads and bridges to help connect our country.

Now we are in an entirely different era, things that I couldn't have even imagined when I saw my father bring home the first VCR I had ever seen and plug it in in my house. Now we have more connected devices on the planet Earth than there are people, and we are in the stone age of the Internet of Things.

What excites me is that I have a partner to my right here who understands that if we in government don't get our act together, we are going to miss out on not only trying to help the private sector flourish in this area, but frankly, we are going to drag down the private sector, because we are going to have agencies within the government that are working in silos and are tripping up and undermining innovations.

I am extraordinarily excited about this panel because you all are on the cutting edge of what is a whole new world, and a world that for me as a guy who comes from the inner city and represented that as mayor, I began to see how connectivity, innovation, and technology, can be a massively democratizing force that can create and expand opportunity, in many ways in the same way as us building the interstate highway system or creating the transcontinental railroad, which the engine, by the way, was built in New Jersey.

So I want to get right to it. I want to thank you all for being here. And a lot of the things that you're going to say are wisdoms that we've tried to put together in the DIGIT Act that the Senator and I have together with two of our other colleagues in a bipartisan fashion.

But I just want to say welcome to Washington. This is really exciting. I don't understand why all the cameras are on the other side of the Capitol talking about some place way over on the other side of the world, and there isn't more press here focusing on this, because this is a panel talking about things that are going to change the life of every American in ways that they cannot imagine.

Thank you very much.

[The prepared statement of Senator Booker follows:]

PREPARED STATEMENT OF CORY BOOKER, U.S. SENATOR FROM NEW JERSEY

Thank you Chairman Fischer for holding this important hearing on the potential for advanced technologies, known as the Internet of Things, to improve the safety and efficiency of our surface transportation systems. In simple terms, the goal of the Internet of Things is to create an environment where physical objects—such as parking meters, cars, and street lights—can talk to each other so that transportation and other systems work better.

The Internet of Things also promises to make cities smarter in how they deliver services to residents.

As the former Mayor of Newark, New Jersey, I know firsthand that our cities face many challenges and that funds are in short supply. The vast majority of a city's budget goes to delivering everyday services like keeping the street lights on, picking up the trash, and repairing aging transportation, water, and energy infrastructure. That's one of the reasons why the Internet of Things is so important to me—because these technologies can help cities deliver everyday services more efficiently and make meaningful improvements to people's quality of life.

For example, in a smart city, the traffic moves more safely and efficiently because signals are timed to allow for rapid buses, safer bike lanes, and complete streets where pedestrians are not an afterthought.

In a smart city, residents from all economic groups have information on all of their transportation options available at their fingertips, so they can find the best way to get to work, to job interviews, or to new opportunities.

In a smart city, even everyday infrastructure such as street lamps, are equipped not only to efficiently light the way for pedestrians, but also to deliver wireless Internet to underserved communities, or to monitor air quality or noise pollution in local neighborhoods.

In a smart city, our ports and freight networks work better because advanced communication technologies allow carriers and shippers to monitor their shipments to keep supply chains moving.

All of these exciting visions are enabled by the Internet of Things.

And this great panel of experts before us today can speak firsthand about the promise of these innovations, as well as some of the challenges that we face in making them happen. To make smart cities a reality, technology developers, city governments, and transportation companies need an environment that encourages experimentation and innovation.

That's why I—along with Senators Fischer, Ayotte, and Schatz—introduced bipartisan legislation known as the ''Developing Innovation and Growing the Internet of Things'' or DIGIT Act. The DIGIT Act will create an environment where innovators have ample access to spectrum and Congress has the information necessary to lower the barriers to building the Internet of Things. The DIGIT Act is just one of several new efforts to challenge cities, companies, and transportation providers to work together to make the United States a global leader in the Internet of Things.

For example, the Department of Transportation recently held its Smart City Challenge, in which cities from across the country developed plans to use this technology to transform their transportation systems. Of the 78 cities that took up the challenge, DOT awarded funding to seven cities to further hone their plans. In the end, the CITY OF X, was awarded $X million to begin implementing their vision for X, Y, and Z. However, all of the cities who participated—including my friends in Newark and Jersey City—will benefit from having developed actionable plans to bring their transportation systems into the 21st Century.

And that's what this hearing is about—leveraging technology to make our transportation infrastructure work better for everyone now, and into the future.

I look forward to hearing from this expert panel about their lessons learned so far in developing the Internet of Things in transportation, and learning what steps we in Congress should take to help foster innovation.

Senator Fischer—thank you again for having the foresight to call this hearing and for being a great partner in encouraging innovation in transportation.

Senator FISCHER. Thank you, Senator Booker.

Don't you just love it when he geeks out?

No, I am also very excited that we get started. So with that, I would like to introduce the panel. We will begin with the Honorable Carlos Monje, the Assistant Secretary for Transportation Policy at the U.S. Department of Transportation.

Welcome, sir. If you would like to give your opening statement?

STATEMENT OF HON. CARLOS MONJE, JR., ACTING UNDER SECRETARY OF TRANSPORTATION FOR POLICY, AND ASSISTANT SECRETARY FOR TRANSPORTATION POLICY, U.S. DEPARTMENT OF TRANSPORTATION

Mr. MONJE. Thank you. Chairman Fischer, Ranking Member Booker, members of the Subcommittee, thank you for inviting me here today.

We are getting to a point in history where data is as important to transportation as asphalt. The Internet of Things has the potential to slash commute times, to eliminate traffic accidents, reduce CO_2 emissions, and reshape communities for the better.

Already, we are beginning to see major advances: connected traffic signals that detect cars and pedestrians to improve safety and speed traffic; wayfinding applications that let commuters pick the most convenient way to get around; and sensors that help traffic engineers fix and detect structural problems.

Soon, we are going to see increased deployment of technologies that will spread out travel demand and nudge travelers to make informed choices. We are going to see revolutionized logistics that include robotics, automation, and truck platooning.

Most thrilling, automated vehicles hold the promise to dramatically reduce deadly crashes and reclaim millions of hours of lost time. The President's Council of Advisors on Science and Technology said that the time regained from not driving could be worth $1.2 trillion a year, not to mention the benefits of reclaiming land from parking spaces.

While we know that this transformation will be driven by the private sector, we are doing our part at U.S. DOT, first by building an enabling regulatory environment; second, by never wavering from our focus on safety, security, privacy, and equity; and third, by investing in key research and tech deployments.

At Secretary Foxx's direction, we are doing everything we can to remove regulatory obstacles to provide the certainty and flexibility needed to encourage innovation.

For instance, NHTSA is systematically reviewing its regulatory framework, making clear to innovators how to seek redress from existing barriers, developing a framework for Federal and State regulators to work together, and identifying needed new regulatory tools.

Our Highway Administration is finalizing guidance to road planners to how to legally and effectively install vehicle infrastructure equipment. The Federal Transit Administration is reviewing its rules to enable transit agencies across the country to participate in the mobility-on-demand revolution.

And as the department enters this brave new world, we are combining the tools we have with the lessons we've learned, starting with a strong partnership with industry and building on a foundation of data and transparency.

We have kept a razor-sharp focus on safety, security, and privacy. We are working closely with the FTC, and we are pursuing connected vehicles in a way that protects consumers from privacy risks and protects vehicles from hacking, tampering, or tracking.

We are also moving aggressively on a number of fronts to bolster cybersecurity. NHTSA has challenged the auto industry to form an information-sharing and analysis center to proactively address cyberthreats. We've collaborated across all corners of the Federal Government to give planners the ability to capture and manage big data in ways that protect the privacy and safety of users.

We are also investing our dollars in a strategic way to fund foundational research, to speed promising technologies to market, and to spur the national conversation on the future of mobility.

FTA's Mobility on Demand program includes an $8 million sandbox, which is going to help public transit agencies explore new ways to partner with emerging service providers, whether that be carpooling, transit on-demand, or bike sharing, to provide better options to their constituents.

FHWA is operating three connected vehicles pilots to speed truck movements in southern Wyoming, to improve pedestrian safety in New York City, and test mobility apps in Tampa. We've developed the Freight Advanced Traveler Information System, FRATIS, which is demonstrating how sensors and data systems can speed the transfer of cargo at the Ports of Los Angeles and Long Beach.

And last week, Secretary Foxx announced the winner of the Smart City Challenge, a national competition to transform one midsize city using advanced data and technology. Columbus, Ohio, will receive $40 million from us, plus a whole lot of support from a host of partners, and the city is going to deploy electronic self-driving shuttles to connect its residents to BRT lines. They're going to put sensors on their city fleet to improve safety. They're going to invest in truck platooning, and make it easier for delivery vehicles to find parking on city streets. And they are integrating their transportation data with other parts of their city, particularly health care scheduling to help address high rates of infant mortality.

Seventy-eight cities applied. Each created a blueprint for the future of transportation on their city streets. And the biggest lesson of the Smart City Challenge is that technology deployment is not an end to itself, but rather a means to build strong communities that create opportunity for all its citizens.

Thank you for the opportunity to discuss the department's visions. Thanks also for this subcommittee's leadership in holding this hearing and introducing legislation to speed planning for the Internet of Things. I'm glad to answer the questions you have.

[The prepared statement of Mr. Monje follows:]

PREPARED STATEMENT OF HON. CARLOS MONJE, JR., ACTING UNDER SECRETARY OF TRANSPORTATION FOR POLICY, AND ASSISTANT SECRETARY FOR TRANSPORTATION POLICY, U.S. DEPARTMENT OF TRANSPORTATION

Chairman Fischer, Ranking Member Booker, and Members of the Subcommittee, thank you for inviting me to appear before you to discuss how the Department of

Transportation is advancing the Internet of Things and its ability to transform communities.

America has led the world in transportation creativity, from the Wright brothers at Kitty Hawk to Ford's Model-T. Today, our ability to innovate continues to be the envy of the world. Over time, government has played a critical role fostering new innovations—the Global Positioning System, the Internet, and the advent of civil aviation are just a few examples of how the government has shaped the market in revolutionary ways. Over the past seven and a half years, the Obama Administration has strengthened our foundation for innovation through key investments and critical reforms to drive technological breakthroughs that will power our economy and inspire the world for generations to come.

Perhaps no sector better captures the imagination about how connectivity can improve the way we move. The potential impacts of fully integrated transportation infrastructure are profound. Zero transportation fatalities. Drastically reduced commute times. Diminished contributions to climate change. We know that over the next 30 years, America's population will grow by 70 million and the freight moving across our roads, rails, pipelines and airports will increase 45 percent. As a nation, we will not be able to build our way out of the growing congestion and all its effects. Instead, we have to be smarter about the capacity we have. Emerging technology has the potential to dramatically improve our lives.

The Wow Factor

- The next generation of mobility technology is in the early stages of deployment, giving us a glimpse of what is to come.
- Connected traffic signals that detect cars and pedestrians in real time, dramatically reducing risks to pedestrians, wait times at empty intersections, and sharing information with the network to anticipate and speed traffic flows across an entire city or region.
- Wayfinding applications that enable commuters to decide instantly the cheapest and most convenient way to get around, whether by reserving a parking space for their own car, activating a carshare vehicle, signing up for a carpool, biking or using public transit.
- Common payment systems that allow users to travel easily across modes and other solutions to help the unbanked and those without cell phones access these services.
- Connected vehicles that soon will help drivers avoid dangerous situations.
- Sensors that help engineers detect pavement and structural bridge problems and fix them before they become less safe and more expensive to repair; and
- Unmanned aerial vehicles (UAV) that can inspect bridges and pavements, observe on-going construction, and monitor and report traffic incidents.

In the immediate future, we anticipate seeing the increased deployment of technologies and access to data that will:

- help transportation planners better track how their networks perform so they can target their road building, prioritize essential roadway services, evaluate the need for truck parking solutions, and offer more responsive transit services;
- help spread out travel demand and encourage more sustainable choices by informing travelers and freight operators, nudging them to optimize and plan their trip slightly differently;
- help automate freight deliveries with robotic loading and unloading, maximize efficiencies along our freight network—including research on the operational and safety impacts of truck platooning;
- provide automated first-and last-mile public transit to encourage transit use and reduce parking needs;
- have the potential to dramatically reduce deadly crashes, cut losses in vehicle and infrastructure damages, and reclaim millions of hours of lost time through the deployment of fully automated vehicles; and
- make transportation projects completely paperless from planning to the post construction phase, saving time and money for State DOTs as well as contractors.

We know that this transformation will be driven by the private sector, and by our state, local and tribal partners, but the Department of Transportation is working to speed the benefits of the IoT, first; by building an enabling regulatory environment; second, by never wavering from our focus on safety, security and privacy; and third, by investing in catalytic research and technology deployments.

Finding Innovative Approaches

As Secretary Foxx has said, DOT is bullish on technology. The degree to which we can anticipate breakthroughs, remove obstacles and streamline efforts to enable innovation could mean the difference between shaping new markets or being subject to them. More than ever, transportation innovation can be restricted by the slow pace of legislation and rulemaking. Rapidly evolving technology will demand government flexibility: regulations may be necessary, but they can also provide the certainty to encourage innovation.

For instance, the National Highway Traffic Safety Administration (NHTSA) is systematically reviewing its current regulatory framework to identify and overcome any provisions that could slow this transformation, including clarifying existing rules, developing a framework for Federal and state regulations, and identifying new regulatory tools that might be required to meet DOT's safety mission in an era of rapidly changing technology. DOT's Volpe Center, on behalf of NHTSA recently completed such an evaluation for highly automated vehicles and found that, while existing regulations pose few regulatory barriers to automated vehicle systems, some design innovations (*e.g.,* the elimination of a steering wheel and foot pedals) could complicate compliance with current standards. Soon, NHTSA will be unveiling the next steps of this framework, which have been informed by our state partners and will be fleshed out in partnership with industry.

In pursuit of a new partnership approach, this past March, NHTSA and the Insurance Institute for Highway Safety announced an historic commitment by 20 automakers representing more than 99 percent of the U.S. auto market to make automatic emergency braking a standard feature on nearly all new cars no later than NHTSA's 2022 reporting year. The unprecedented commitment means that this important safety technology will be available to more consumers more quickly than would be possible through the traditional regulatory process.

One of the most exciting areas that the Department is fully engaged in is pushing forward the safe deployment of connected and automated safety technologies in vehicles. The Department is leading the way forward in integrating both connected and automated vehicle technologies in a way that brings the benefits we all hear about. These include crash avoidance, reduced energy consumption and vehicle emissions, reduced travel times, improved travel time reliability and multi-modal connectivity, and improved transportation system efficiency and accessibility, particularly for persons with disabilities and the growing aging population. For example, the Federal Highway Administration (FHWA) is supporting research on systems to make travel easier for blind pedestrians and other travelers under the Accessible Transportation Technologies Research Initiative (ATTRI). In addition, FHWA will issue guidance and technical support tools on how to invest in infrastructure that enables the connected systems which will, in turn, increase safety, enhance mobility, deliver reliability and cut our carbon footprint.

Another exciting initiative is taking place at the Federal Transit Administration (FTA). The agency is administering the Mobility-on-Demand (MOD) ''Sandbox,'' an effort to bring non-traditional partners together to promote enhanced, multimodal mobility concepts using advanced technologies and new business models for providing improved transportation service. One effect of the Sandbox will be to encourage multimodal connectivity and system interoperability so that transportation resources are interconnected and accessible to all potential users. The FTA understands that the best way to answer the question of whether new operational models might work is through real-world demonstrations that can measure the impacts on regional transportation system networks to see what the net benefits to travelers and local economies really are. Running these demonstrations will also allow the Department to examine how rules and regulations impact the implementation of MOD services.

Still, clear rules of the road that ensure safeguards to protect people must be put in place, as government seeks to spur innovation without compromising safety and privacy.

Security and Privacy

The Department has worked hard to support the design and deployment of connected vehicle technologies, such as vehicle-to-vehicle (V2V) communications, in a manner that protects consumers from unwarranted privacy risks and prevents unauthorized access to data. As envisioned, the connected vehicle system will contain multiple technical controls to help mitigate potential privacy risks and prevent tampering with equipment or data. For example, V2V broadcast messages will not contain data that identifies the vehicle or its owner. We also are working with privacy experts to develop algorithms to sanitize connected vehicle data sets, which will enable the Department to make connected vehicle data available publicly without putting consumer privacy at risk. Going forward, the Department plans to work with the Federal Trade Commission and stakeholders to ensure that we develop regulatory strategies and guidance in the area of consumer data privacy.

The Department of Transportation has spent time and resources understanding the nature and implications of cyber security. Since 2012, NHTSA has engaged the potential cyber security threats to automobiles through a diverse set of actions. Our approach includes:

- Encouraging the automotive industry to form an Information Sharing and Analysis Center to help the industry proactively and uniformly address cybersecurity threats, while challenging automakers to adopt proactive safety principles and develop best practices that enhance automotive cybersecurity;
- Collaborating proactively with other government agencies—including the Defense Advanced Research Projects Agency (DARPA), Department of Homeland Security (DHS), National Institute of Standards and Technology (NIST) and National Science Foundation (NSF)—as well as with vehicle manufacturers, automotive suppliers, and the security research community to protect against cyber threats and potential vulnerabilities; and
- Continuing to execute fundamental research aimed at improving the cybersecurity posture of automobiles with a focus on understanding real-time intrusion detection and response measures. We are also assessing solutions and sharing findings broadly to ensure that once a potential vulnerability or a hacking technique is identified, information about the issue and potential solutions is quickly shared with other stakeholders.

In expanding the use of drones the Federal Aviation Administration (FAA) laid out a responsible path with their Small Unmanned Aircraft System (sUAS) rule that is the first set of nationally uniform regulations for the commercial, educational and public use of unmanned aircraft. Building off the recently released UAS privacy best practices developed with industry in a Department of Commerce led multistakeholder convening, the Administration is launching a new privacy education campaign to encourage pilots, companies and others address the privacy implications of these new technologies.

We also recognize that major advances will be needed in Big Data management and analytics, in order to not be overwhelmed by the sheer volume of data. To meet this challenge, Secretary Foxx has called on all corners of the Department—particularly the Intelligent Transportation Systems (ITS) Joint Program Office (JPO)—to focus on managing and providing transportation big data to support new paradigms of data-driven operations. The ITS–JPO is funding multi-modal enterprise data management initiatives focusing on enabling effective data capture from ITS-enabled technologies, including connected passenger, transit, and commercial vehicles; mobile devices; and infrastructure, in ways that protect the privacy of users.

Making Catalyzing Investments

In addition to the communications programs with which you are familiar—the Next Generation Air Traffic Control System (NextGen), V2V and vehicle-to-infrastructure (V2I) communications, wireless roadside inspections (WRI) for trucks and buses, and Positive Train Control (PTC)—we are making key investments that will speed a future in which all of our vehicles, road infrastructure, and even pedestrians are more safely connected.

The FTA and ITS–JPO are co-managing the MOD Research Program, including grants for the MOD Sandbox initiative to help public transit providers adopt new technologies, partner with emerging service providers and provide better transportation options to their constituents.

And, the ITS–JPO and FHWA continue to work on the three Connected Vehicle Pilot Deployment sites to speed safe and efficient truck movement along I–80 in southern Wyoming, improve vehicle flow and pedestrian safety in high-priority corridors in New York City, and deploy multiple safety and mobility applications on and in proximity to reversible freeway lanes in Tampa. The Department continues to collaborate with the private sector on the Freight Advanced Traveler Information Systems (FRATIS) demonstration project.

Through a partnership with the Port of Los Angeles, the Port of Long Beach and their private sector supply chain operators, FRATIS aims to establish a neutral benchmark showing benefits from improved operations, including measureable gains in port performance. This demonstration project is yielding improved on-time arrival for cargo pickup appointments, reduced truck waiting time at port terminals, decreased emissions, and improved fuel consumption.

FHWA also is supporting research on sensor systems that monitor and predict structural and pavement conditions. As these systems mature, they will aid asset owners in maintaining a state of good repair for legacy and new elements of the highway transportation system.

In December 2015, Secretary Foxx launched the *Smart City Challenge*—a national competition to implement bold, data-driven ideas that demonstrate the use of advanced data and intelligent transportation systems technologies to make our network safer, easier, and more reliable in one mid-sized city. The Department is partnering with Paul G. Allen's Vulcan Inc., NXP® Semiconductors, Amazon Web Services, Mobileye, Autodesk and Alphabet's Sidewalk Labs to provide the winning city with up to $40 million plus $10 million from Vulcan, and access to multiple technologies to support the Smart City demonstration. Perhaps more important, the Smart City Challenge is bringing together people, industries and sectors that have rarely communicated before, all jointly addressing urban mobility issues in a way that is more sustainable, more equitable, and safer than ever before.

Nearly every mid-sized city in America—78 cities—answered the call by creating blueprints for the future of transportation today on their city streets. The seven finalist cities—Austin, Columbus, Denver, Kansas City, Pittsburgh, Portland, and San Francisco—proposed first-of-a-kind use of these new technologies to solve the real-world challenges facing cities today. From self-driving shuttles that could cut in half the commute from underserved neighborhoods to job centers, to the use of smart sensors to accelerate freight delivery while improving safety. More than 150 diverse industry and non-profit partners have pledged more than $500 million in re- sources, technology solutions, and support to help carry out these Smart City plans.

- *Austin, TX:* The fastest growing city in the Nation with over 100 new residents a day, Austin faces unique challenges with growing congestion and increasing commutes. To target the challenges facing its commuters, Austin has proposed to remake the traditional ''park-and-ride'' into a ''one-stop shop'' with even more mobility options, including public transit buses, trains, car share, bike share, automated vehicles, and connected vehicles, to be strategically situated near community health centers, the area community college, housing developments, and the airport.

- *Columbus, OH:* The city proposed to deploy three electric self-driving shuttles to connect a new bus rapid transit center to a retail district, connecting more residents to jobs, and to use data analytics to improve health care access in a neighborhood that currently has an infant mortality rate four times that of the national average, allowing them to provide improved transportation options to those most in need of prenatal care.

- *Denver, CO:* Situated at the crossroads of three nationally important freight highways, Denver is applying its pioneering spirit to accelerate freight while improving safety. With partners like FedEx, Peloton, and UPS, Denver is equipping trucks with V2V communication technology to optimize routing and traffic signals and to experiment with connected, autonomous truck platooning, accelerating freight while reducing the impact on low-income neighborhoods that bear the brunt of this traffic flow today.

- *Kansas City, MO:* Kansas City proposed to revitalize a historically black and underserved community by installing ubiquitous public Wi-Fi along sidewalks and on new electric, connected public buses, including on self-driving shuttles connecting underserved areas with the existing streetcar route. Each bus stop will have large-screen, state-of-the-art kiosks to help residents access transportation information and will be equipped with voice-activated wayfinding technology to help the visually impaired navigate the city's streets.

- *Pittsburgh, PA:* Pittsburgh is proposing to cut in half the time it takes workers from Hazelwood, a historically underserved community, to reach the city's urban jobs core by partnering with Carnegie Mellon, a pioneer of self-driving technology, to construct a thirty minute loop for autonomous shuttles. Throughout the city, Pittsburgh will also deploy state-of-the-art traffic signal technology—proven to reduce congestion at street lights by forty percent—to significantly reduce travel and idle time for all residents.

- *Portland, OR:* Portland proposed to launch the Nation's first bulk-buy program for used electric vehicles (EV) to put affordable EVs in the hands of low-income drivers in demonstration corridors and promote electric car sharing and electric bike sharing in low-income communities. At the same time, Portland is partnering on autonomous vehicle demonstrations from campus shuttles and airport buses to self-driving taxis and tractor trailers. Portland is also developing a smart housing app with real transparency about the true cost of an apartment, including both rent and transportation costs.

- *San Francisco, CA:* San Francisco has set a goal of eliminating one out of every ten single occupant car trips by shifting travelers onto carpooling and public transit. To increase uptake of innovative carpooling and ridesharing models, San Francisco envisions a system of new carpooling high-occupancy vehicle (HOV) lanes and reserved curbside pickup areas. In addition, San Francisco has proposed using self-driving cars to shuttle passengers for the first and last mile onto public transit. The city, long a leader in innovation, has also proposed sharing its learnings with a tech transfer network of 50 cities and 25,000 transportation professionals.

While the City of Columbus was named the winner, we are excited to see the innovation in their proposals and even more excited that 78 cities reached out to develop new local and regional partnerships, with hundreds of partners beyond those the Department has gathered.

Through Smart Cities, the Department has also developed new Federal relationships—most notably with the Department of Energy's SMART Mobility consortium and with NIST's Internet of Things-Enabled Smart City Framework– so that we can continue to move forward with the best knowledge of new technologies and innovative transportation solutions.

Altogether, the Department is using its dollars in a strategic way to fund primary research, speed promising technologies to market, convene unlikely partners at the local level and spur on the national conversation on the future of mobility.

Using Technology to Build the Communities We Want

The biggest lesson of the Smart City Challenge is that technology deployment is not an end to itself, but rather a means to build strong communities that create opportunity for all of its citizens. The Federal Government has focused on the IoT's potential to make our national network more efficient, and to make our transportation system safer, but the 78 communities that applied to be part of the Smart City Challenge each articulated a vision for how connected infrastructure and enhanced mobility options will make the lives of their citizens better.

Together, the Smart City applicants are showing us what it means to think beyond the traditional transportation modes, and embrace the surprising and disruptive innovations coming from the private sector. These technological shifts could help increase access to opportunity in neglected and underserved communities and meet our environmental commitments at the same time.

As technology continues to advance, the Department, and all levels of governance, will need to anticipate, accommodate, and incentivize innovation; and to understand and mitigate the risks associated with new technologies to ensure that our transportation system remains safe, reliable, efficient, equitable and secure.

Thank you for the opportunity to discuss the Department's vision and activities related to the Internet of Things. I am glad to answer any questions you may have.

Senator FISCHER. Thank you very much.

Next, we have Ms. Seleta Reynolds, who is the General Manager of the Los Angeles Department of Transportation.

Welcome.

STATEMENT OF SELETA REYNOLDS, GENERAL MANAGER, LOS ANGELES DEPARTMENT OF TRANSPORTATION; AND PRESIDENT, NATIONAL ASSOCIATION OF CITY TRANSPORTATION OFFICIALS (NACTO)

Ms. REYNOLDS. Thank you. Good morning, Chairwoman Fischer, Ranking Member Booker. Thank you so much to you as well as Chairman Thune and Ranking Member Nelson for the opportunity to come and speak with you today.

My name is Seleta Reynolds. I am the General Manager of the Los Angeles Department of Transportation. I'm also the President of the National Association of City Transportation Officials, or NACTO.

I would like to describe where we are, where we are going, and the challenges that we face.

The City of Los Angeles is investing millions of dollars into our transportation system to try and evolve our reputation as the car capital of the world into the capital of one of the most modern sophisticated transportation systems in the world.

Technology doesn't just change the outcomes in our cities. It changes us as well. So it is important for us to stay focused on people first, if we want to get to the best and brightest outcomes that are possible.

If we rely solely on the private side, those benefits may only land where they benefit the wealthiest among us. Our role is to make sure that the rising tide lifts all boats.

Back in 1984, Los Angeles hosted the Olympics. The hottest gadget was the Sony Discman, and we invested in an interconnected system of signals called ATSAC that relied on algorithms to move cars and people through our streets—in fact, more than any other city in the country.

Today, we rely on painted signs and signals to speak to drivers. In the future, that information will go directly to the vehicles themselves. These digital interfaces between the city's infrastructure and the passengers' vehicles will improve the safe flow of people and goods, light and heavy rail, and even equestrians across the city.

More than 2 million people today in Los Angeles are using apps to navigate our streets. Earlier this year, we launched a Go LA app. This app allows you to choose a cheaper, faster, greener way to get from point A to point B. We give sort of a level playing field and a mobility marketplace, and let the consumer make the choice about how they want to travel around our city.

The next step is to evolve that into a universal payment platform where people can actually make that choice, pay for that choice, and be on their way all in the palm of their hand.

We are currently launching electric vehicle car-sharing in the heart of our city. While car-sharing markets have evolved in some areas, we are deliberately making this accessible to people who stand to benefit the most. We are investing public dollars to bring in private sector investment.

City government has a powerful role to play to ensure that new services are understandable, legible, and accessible. We embed the needs of older adults, people unfamiliar with smart phones, or those who don't have bank cards. We partner with community groups to help people navigate possible language and cultural barriers.

We are also preparing a pilot of on-demand public transit, and requesting funds to upgrade signals and streets to, for example, hold a signal at red if it detects a driver about to run the light, turn signals green for transit emergency vehicles, and alert transit operators to the right speeds to get a green wave. And we are requesting proposals to develop what we call mobility hubs throughout the city at major transit stops to bring car share, bike share, and real-time transit information to travelers.

Our interest is to use technology to treat people with hospitality. We want it to be a convener and not a splitter.

Older technologies are also reemerging in new and interesting ways. We are outfitting our city buses with Wi-Fi and real-time location updating, and becoming safer and more convenient.

Bicycles are increasingly being electrified and app-ified to be an easier, safer, healthier and even more fun way to travel—maybe most importantly, a more fun way to travel.

Signals are becoming smarter to help emergency responders in transit be more efficient than ever before.

I want to underscore that the technologies of today are not static, and we don't want to become too wedded to one mode or pick winners and losers or ignore the real equity issues that we face. Autonomous vehicles may reduce the number of human errors occurring, but also have the potential for increased traffic, emissions from additional driving, on-street congestion, and could be very expensive to own.

Technologies such as alternative fuels and shared mobility will change the funding framework. We hope that we can work closely with our partners at U.S. DOT to continue to have a conversation about initiative funding and direct aid to cities, about realigned and flexible funding, about requiring technology to be built into transportation at the most fundamental levels, and to pivot from expansion to modernization and management. So fixing it first and making our infrastructure smarter, rather than continuing to invest in expansion.

Data-sharing is key to us; ongoing investment into mass transit like high-capacity rails, because one of the most precious resources in cities will continue to be space; and preparing our work force.

As you can see, LA is an exciting place to be right now. We know that great cities generate traffic, but traffic doesn't generate great cities. Technology has the power to help communities achieve their visions, taking back public space from congestion, traffic, and parking.

I want to thank Chairwoman Fischer, Ranking Member Booker, and the Committee members for the opportunity to testify. Our cities are changing perhaps nowhere as quickly as Los Angeles, and we need the Federal Government to work with us on funding, standardizing, and exploring the future.

[The prepared statement of Ms. Reynolds follows:]

PREPARED STATEMENT OF SELETA REYNOLDS, GENERAL MANAGER, LOS ANGELES DEPARTMENT OF TRANSPORTATION; AND PRESIDENT, NATIONAL ASSOCIATION OF CITY TRANSPORTATION OFFICIALS (NACTO)

Good morning Chairman Fischer, Ranking Member Booker and committee members.

I am Seleta Reynolds, General Manager of the Los Angeles Department of Transportation. I am also President of the National Association of City Transportation Officials, also known as NACTO. It is an honor to be here to discuss the Internet of things transportation, at the city level. I would like to describe where we are, where we are going, and the challenges that we face.

The City of Los Angeles is investing millions of dollars into promoting a modern, multimodal transportation system; to evolve from our infamous, 20th Century reputation as the car capital of the U.S. toward the most sophisticated, modern transportation system in the world. Technology doesn't just change the outcome in our cities and country; it changes those who use it as well. We must be smart and focused on people first in order to achieve the best of technology's entry into transportation.

From ridesharing to micro-transit, new products emerge daily. Therefore, the city is making a home for current, future and evolving modes in the mobility market-place. In the marketplace the city will not pick winners or losers, but create an incubator that nurtures the best and safest ways to travel. We are not wedded to what exists today, but seek to be prepared for what is coming tomorrow. The menu of travel options also ensures that should one mode become disabled, travelers are not paralyzed.

Safety, environmental quality, equity, affordability, efficiency and quality of life all have benefits to achieve from technology.

If we rely solely on the private side, these benefits may only land where they benefit the wealthiest among us. Our role to play in making sure the rising tide lifts all boats.

Yesterday and Today

Los Angeles made an effective first pass at using technology in transportation management in 1984 when it hosted the Summer Olympics. In the era of floppy disks L.A. pioneered a system called ATSAC that used algorithms to optimize the movement of vehicles through streets. Today L.A. *is* looking to upgrade that network to provide digital services to private, commercial, and public vehicles and include recommended speeds and safety data. Today we rely solely upon painted signs along the streets to tell drivers how fast to drive, tomorrow this information will be communicated directly to a vehicle from the infrastructure. These digital interfaces between the city's infrastructure and the passenger's vehicles will improve the safe flow of people and goods, light and heavy rail, and even equestrians across *the* City.

Today more than 2 million people in L.A. are using apps to navigate the streets. Earlier this year we launched a ''Go LA'' app. This app shows travelers the many options for moving across Los Angeles organized by whether the user is trying to get somewhere faster, cheaper, or greener. For example, I can select a destination and be provided with detailed options that include walking, biking, transit, taxi, TNC and driving information. It may take me 25 minutes to walk, but I'll burn 100 calories and it won't cost me a dime. Another option presented might be a carpool trip of 5 minutes, $4, 10 pounds of carbon emissions, and burning 15 calories. We give all modes an equal opportunity and allow the consumer to decide. The next step is to provide seamless payment—one way to pay for any transit mode including bike share.

We are currently launching electric vehicle car sharing the heart of our city. While car-sharing markets have evolved in some areas, we are deliberately making this accessible to people who stand to benefit the most. We are investing public dollars and securing private sector investment as well. City government has a powerful role to play in offsetting risks and promoting investment in traditionally underserved or low-income areas. We have an obligation to ensure that new services are understandable, legible, and accessible to people. This includes considering those that are older, unfamiliar with smartphones, or that may not have a bank cards. We also have to partner with community groups to help people navigate possible language and cultural barriers.

We are also preparing a pilot of on-demand public transit and requesting funds to upgrade signals and streets to, for example, hold a signal at red if it detects a driver about to run the light, turn signals green for transit and emergency vehicles, and alert transit operators to the right speeds to get a green wave. And we are requesting proposals to develop what we call Mobility Hubs throughout the city at major transit stops to bring bikeshare, carshare, and real-time transit information to travelers. Our interest is to use technology to treat people with hospitality and convene as many choices as possible for them.

Older technologies are also re-emerging in new and interesting ways. City buses are getting Wi-Fi and real-time location updating, as well as becoming even safer and more convenient. Bicycles are being increasingly electrified and app-ified to be an easier, safer, healthier, and even more fun way to travel. Signals are becoming smarter to help emergency responders and transit be more efficient than ever before.

The Future and the Role of Government

I would like to underscore that the technologies of today are not static nor should we become overly wedded to one mode or ignore very real equity issues. For example, autonomous vehicles may reduce the number of human errors occurring, but also have the potential for increased traffic, emissions from additional driving, on-street congestion and could be very expensive to own. Technologies such as alternative fuels and shared use mobility will change the funding framework. Federal regulators should be encouraged to approach the future with these considerations:

- Initiative Funding and Direct Aid to Cities. Direct aid significantly reduces the overhead and administrative costs often associated with Federal funds. We especially appreciate the acknowledgement in recent grants that federalized procurement requirements will slow down rapid pilots and partnerships. U.S. DOT and DOE have been terrific pioneers with the Smart Cities and ARPA-e NEXTCAR programs. These, along with the recommendations from the White House PCAST report published earlier this year on urban development districts, will greatly help American cities move with technology changes. They help cities come to the table to create partnerships with private companies.
- Realigned and Flexible Funding. The tradition of using gas taxes and parking revenues to fund transportation initiatives will become obsolete. Connected autonomous vehicles may not need to park. Electric vehicles don't use gas. Instead, we expect to see digital services provided to users with fees for levels of service. Additionally, new modes like electric powered, shared automated vehicles require regulatory and funding streams that are convoluted under current programs.
- Require tech to be built into transportation at the most fundamental levels. Infrastructure to vehicle communication capability should be required in all transportation construction from Bus Rapid Transit and roads to bike lanes and freeway construction.
- Pivot from expansion to modernization and management to account for the impacts of automated vehicles. Existing roadway space will be used more efficiently through connected technology, making new capacity irrelevant in the near future. Transportation planning at all levels should refocus on modernizing existing expressways with instrumentation for new technology for traffic management. Traffic management will remain a public sector function even in a future dominated by private mobility providers.
- Data sharing: the need for accurate and timely data underlies everything that is changing, especially in the digital world. Our access to the data needed for planning and operating cities is increasingly siloed. The Federal Government can be a strong proponent of open data, data sharing and storage, and, of course, data standards. Data-sharing requirements can substantially reduce the millions of dollars spent annually on technologically primitive data collection, both from regular traffic operation and from traffic crashes.
- Ongoing investment into mass transit like high-capacity rail. One of the most precious resource in cities is space. Even if automation allows us to be more efficient and move more vehicles, we will not have the curb space to accommodate continuous pick-ups and drop-offs. We will always need an urban network for people and possibly, for goods in the future.
- Preparing our workforce—We must proactively give people the skills to be able to consume and understand data and technology for better planning, management and project evaluation.

As you can see, L.A. is an exciting place to be right now. We are on the cutting edge for implementation and regulation of technology in infrastructure. We have an important role to play in protecting our residents and businesses and to support the mobility marketplace. We must be at the table in planning for an increasingly automated future. Future visioning for automated vehicles should begin from the inside out, from the centers of our economy, looking at land use as well as transportation. Theories of automation that focus simply on fitting more vehicles into an expressway lane every hour are beginning from the product of the economy rather than the motor of the economy. *Great cities generate traffic; traffic does not generate great cities.* Technology has the power to help communities achieve their visions both for transportation and for land use, taking public space back from congestion, traffic and parking.

I want to again thank Chairman Fischer, Ranking Member Booker and the Committee members for the opportunity to testify today. Our cities are changing, perhaps nowhere as quickly as Los Angeles, and we need the Federal Government to work with us on funding, standardizing, and exploring the future.

Senator FISCHER. Thank you very much.

Next, I'm going to go to Mr. Doug Davis, who is the Senior Vice President and General Manager of Intel Corporation. Welcome.

STATEMENT OF DOUG DAVIS, SENIOR VICE PRESIDENT AND GENERAL MANAGER, INTEL CORPORATION

Mr. DAVIS. Good morning, Chairwoman Fischer, Ranking Member Booker, and Senator Ayotte. I really appreciate the opportunity to be able to testify this morning.

As head of Intel's IoT group, I am responsible for the company's IoT strategy and the underlying technologies, and all of that includes transportation and automotive. Intel has been delivering integrated or embedded computing for things for over 35 years. The investment, innovations and standard leadership we've driven during that time provide the foundational elements of that IoT strategy.

Intel defines IoT quite simply as devices which are securely connected through the network to the data center or cloud. And it is the data from these things that can be shared and analyzed to solve problems.

In fact, we believe that security is the foundation of the Internet of Things. Our hardware and software are designed from the beginning to be secure. We build security into the transistors or the way that we design our chips.

In addition, we build security into the layers of software in these things as well as the way in which data is moved from those things into the cloud. So we fully realize that safety and security are essential for the promise of the Internet of Things to be fulfilled.

Transportation is one of the most promising sectors in the IoT. In fact, IDC has projected that global revenue from the transportation sector will reach $325 billion just by the year 2018.

By converting vast amounts of data into meaningful, actionable intelligence, the IoT will help support solutions in terms of transportation safety, efficiency, mobility, and some of the infrastructure challenges. Indeed, innovations in the transportation sector are at the heart of the global race for IoT leadership, and that race is really competitive.

In addition to the U.S., we see self-driving car trials on public roads in the U.K., China, Germany, Switzerland, Japan, Sweden, South Korea, the Netherlands, and in Dubai, and that is just a handful. It's kind of a big handful. But this is a big deal for U.S. technology leadership.

Autonomous vehicles require highly advanced sensors to see the things around the car: a variety of technologies to enable collision avoidance; powerful in-vehicle computing and capabilities to calculate those vehicle trajectories; and secure, high-speed ultrareliable connectivity back to the advanced data centers of the cloud.

These autonomous vehicles must become the ultimate learning machines. They are going to need to be able to make smarter and safer decisions than even the most skilled human driver.

In fact, cars will become known as data centers on wheels. And in order for this to occur, these autonomous and 5G technologies will evolve at the pace of innovation, because they are going to have vast global industry support and rapid marketplace adoption.

Autonomous vehicles will also improve our efficiency and productivity, as I think has already been mentioned a few times. The average American commuter spends 38 hours per year stuck in traffic, which collectively costs the U.S. economy about \$121 billion per year in just wasted time and fuel.

The U.S. freight transportation industry alone could save \$168 billion per year in fuel reduction, not to mention the benefit in reducing harmful emissions.

For the U.S. to lead the world in IoT transportation and capture these vast economic and societal benefits that a modernized transportation infrastructure, autonomous vehicles, and 5G connectivity will deliver, Intel recommends that policymakers collaborate with the high-tech and transportation industries to develop an ambitious national IoT transportation strategy based on five principles. Number one, prioritize safety to reduce the number and severity of crashes. Number two, prioritize security from the outset. Three, promote technology neutrality by relying on marketplace innovation and competition. Encourage open, global standards based on transportation platforms to enable a commercialization path that is scalable, interoperable, and reusable across deployments. And then finally, number five, invest in public-private partnerships. That will help launch and scale future looking transportation testbeds, especially in areas like 5G, to develop trusted data and secure computing, machine learning, open standards, and, of course, security.

So I want to thank you for this opportunity to share Intel's policy recommendations for a U.S. IoT transportation leadership, and I look forward to questions a little bit later.

[The prepared statement of Mr. Davis follows:]

PREPARED STATEMENT OF DOUG DAVIS, SENIOR VICE PRESIDENT AND GENERAL MANAGER, INTEL CORPORATION

Intel Corporation (Intel) respectfully submits this statement for the record in conjunction with the Senate Commerce, Science & Transportation Committee, Surface Transportation and Merchant Marine Infrastructure, Safety and Security Subcommittee, hearing on "How the Internet of Things (IoT) Can Bring U.S. Transportation and Infrastructure into the 21st Century." Our statement focuses on the opportunity to unleash the enormous potential of the IoT to enable vastly improved transportation safety, mobility and efficiency—and, in doing so, seize a leadership opportunity for the U.S. by ensuring that the Nation's intelligent transportation technology evolves at the forefront of innovation.

Witness: Doug Davis is the Senior Vice President and General Manager of Intel's worldwide IoT Group (IoTG). Doug has been an Intel employee for 32 years, and began his career as a product engineer in the company's Military and Special Products Division. Over the last decade, Doug has run Intel's worldwide Embedded and Communications Group, managed wafer factory operations, and now leads the IoT Group. This organization is responsible for the company's IoT strategy and solutions—consisting of hardware, software, security and services across a wide range of market segments, including transportation, manufacturing, healthcare, retail, smart home, smart buildings and smart cities. For more than 30 years, Intel has made significant investments, driven exciting innovations, led standards activities, and supported what has evolved to become the IoT. At Intel, we like to say that the IoT is an overnight transformation thirty years in the making.

Background

The Internet of Things. At its simplest, the IoT is: "Things" (devices) securely connected through a network to the cloud (datacenter), from which data can be shared and analyzed to create value (solve problems). The IoT enables us to connect "things" like phones, appliances, machinery and cars to the Internet, share and analyze the data generated by these things, and extract meaningful insights that create new opportunities and solve problems. These opportunities are extensive and exciting with the ability to transform entire industries and our lives for the better. The IoT encompasses two major segments: Consumer IoT and Industrial IoT. The "Consumer IoT" connects devices like game consoles, smart TVs, household appliances, wearables and smart phones. The "Industrial IoT" connects devices in industrial environments like factory equipment, security cameras, medical devices and digital signs.

Transportation is one of the most promising sectors for the IoT. By converting vast amounts of data into meaningful and actionable intelligence, the IoT can help solve many of modern society's automotive safety, transportation efficiency, mobility, and infrastructure challenges. The IoT is rapidly enabling innovations like connected cars, "smart" fleet management, intelligent transportation infrastructure and, of course, self-driving (autonomous) cars. Notably, almost half of Americans aspire to live in a driverless city where cars, buses, and trains operate intelligently and automatically without people driving them, and over one-third expect a driverless city by 2024.[1] A policy framework that harnesses the full potential of these transformational IoT opportunities in the automotive and transportation sector is critical to U.S. economic leadership and productivity in the 21st century.

Intel Leadership in IoT Transportation. As an IoT leader, Intel is committed to driving innovation across all market sectors, with a significant focus on IoT transportation. We are collaborating with policymakers, automakers, suppliers, academia, and cities worldwide—utilizing the IoT to accelerate innovation. Intel is collaborating with our automotive industry partners and governments that seek to not only reimagine the car, but also restructure the idea of transportation as a whole.

To realize the full potential of this new vision, industry must undertake the appropriate and comprehensive testing to ensure that all systems operate flawlessly. Consequently, Intel is building Centers of Excellence (CoEs) to road test autonomous vehicles in our home states of Arizona, California, Oregon and California, as well as Germany.[2] Working with the automotive industry, our CoEs will enable improvements in AV development by gathering data needed to build the machine learning models that will provide the intelligence for these vehicles. We're focusing on what it will take to realize safe, secure, fully autonomous driving, and for vehicles to reliably communicate with each other and the world around them. We are exploring how valuable data can bring new services to market and how smart human-machine interfaces can make autonomous driving intuitive and enjoyable.

For example, we are partnering with automakers to enable platforms with fundamental advanced driver assist features like lane-keeping assistance, collision warning, and automated parking assist,[3] which are early capabilities on the path to self-driving cars.[4] We also are helping businesses use IoT technology to optimize fleet management and freight transport, using real-time data analytics to make drivers safer and more efficient while reducing fuel consumption. We are also partnering with city governments to deliver cutting-edge IoT transportation infrastructure solutions like intelligent traffic management (using advanced data analytics to enable integrated transportation coordination, emergency traffic response, and congestion reduction)[5] and enhanced public transportation experiences (using real-time interactive digital signage to make multi-modal transit easier and more engaging for citizens).[6]

Intel's Vision for IoT in Transportation. Intel's vision for the future of transportation is one of zero accidents, mobility for all, environmental sustainability, reduced congestion, increased efficiency and *innovation that evolves at the pace of technology to ensure U.S. global leadership.* We are making large investments[7] to enable a future of autonomous vehicles with highly advanced sensors; connected cars using advanced cellular technology like 5G (5th generation cellular) for real-time vehicle-to-vehicle (V2V) collision avoidance; powerful in-vehicle computing capabilities to deliver driver strategy and trajectory computing and self-driving capabilities; and secure, high-speed, ultra-reliable communications with advanced data centers in the cloud. All of this will be driven by the IoT and will transform our lives and economies for the better.

---

[1] *The Vote Is In,* Intel Corp. (Feb. 2014), *http://newsroom.intel.com/community/intelnewsroom/blog/2014/02/10/the-vote-is-in-citizens-support-smart-cities-with-driverless-cars-public-service-drones-and-surroundings-that-sense-activities.*

[2] Intel Labs: *http://www.intel.eu/content/www/eu/en/research/intel-labs-europe.html*

[3] ADAS Demo: *http://www.intel.com/content/www/us/en/automotive/advanced-driver-assistance-systems-video.html*

[4] *Self-Driving Car Technology and Computing Requirements,* Intel Corp. *http://www.intel.com/content/www/us/en/automotive/driving-safety-advanced-driver-assistance-systems-self-driving-technology-paper.html.*

[5] Intelligent Traffic Management: *https://www.youtube.com/watch?v=M0ZN8El6lfY*

[6] Real-Time Interactive Transit Displays: *http://www.intel.com/content/www/us/en/intelligent-systems/tech-today/transportation-digital-signage-video.html.*

[7] *Intel Bulking Up Safety and Security of Self-Driving Car Efforts,* Fortune (April 2016) ("Intel Self-Driving Car investments"), *http://fortune.com/2016/04/05/intel-self-driving-car/.*

With the advent of new business models like transportation-as-a-service and the growth of the car sharing economy, the transportation sector is poised to make the leap from technologies and business models grounded in the 20th Century to exciting and empowering technologies firmly anchored in the 21st Century. To successfully compete in the forward-looking global economy, U.S. policymakers must enable a transportation ecosystem that is safe, secure, flexible and interoperable. Global leadership will accrue to those markets that address these goals in the most efficient manner possible.

The challenges for the stakeholder industries are numerous. For example, industry must profitably transition from its current legacy business models to business models that focus less on the human as a ''driver.'' Technology industry suppliers also must pivot to intelligently utilize increasing amounts of data, while addressing the needs of two vastly different generations of consumers—baby boomers who want to maintain mobility and millennials who are challenging the status quo of vehicle ownership. We must adapt as new technologies become the foundation of our transportation ecosystem.

Of particular importance to the stakeholder industries will be how the U.S. Government addresses some of the key foundational technologies that will serve as the core architecture for future capabilities. Most significantly, policymakers should be aware that it is widely expected that 5G cellular (the rapidly emerging successor to today's 4G) will be a foundational technology for the IoT overall and critical to the success of IoT in transportation. For the U.S. to lead in the global IoT transportation future, it is vital that the Nation's transportation strategy recognizes the global marketplace direction and enormous global industry investment in 5G—and that the U.S. pragmatically invest its own limited Federal resources in 5G to keep pace with the transportation industry worldwide.

So what do we mean by 5G, how does it impact the transportation sector specifically, and why does it matter so much? Advanced cellular communications such as next generation 5G technology offer uniquely superior characteristics that are critical for V2V real-time collision avoidance: very low latency (especially in dense vehicle environments),[8] ultra-high reliability, consistent safety prioritization,[9] very high speeds, advanced security, and cost effectiveness to enable scale—and therefore *many more saved lives.* This next generation of cellular also will have the backing of huge global private industry investment and strong consumer demand which propels technologies to the forefront and enables them to evolve at the pace of innovation, which will be key for the long term evolution of IoT solutions.

Evidence of the global race to secure leadership in this space is everywhere and should be viewed by U.S. policymakers as both a wakeup call as well as a challenge to move intelligently and swiftly. Leading examples include 5G deployments that are underway for the 2018 FIFA World Cup in Russia[10] and the 2018 Winter Olympics in PyeongChang, South Korea,[11] followed by the 2020 Summer Olympics in Tokyo, Japan.[12] Moreover, *5G transportation use cases—and specifically V2V safety real-time collision avoidance—already have been demonstrated* in major countries, with more following suit this year. For example, Japanese mobile operator NTT DOCOMO (along with Nokia, Samsung, Ericsson, Fujitsu and Huawei) successfully conducted 5G vehicle trials in actual-use environments in 2015.[13] Also in 2015, Deutsche Telecom (along with Continental, Fraunhofer ESK, and Nokia) successfully demonstrated ''near-5G'' communication between vehicles via the cellular LTE network on the 'Autobahn A9 motorway testbed' in Germany.[14] And Korean mobile

[8] *Letter Report: Review of the Status of the Dedicated Short-Range Communications Technology and Applications [Draft] Report to Congress,* TRB at 5–6 (April 2015), *http://onlinepubs.trb.org/onlinepubs/reports/DSRC\April\28\2015.pdf.*

[9] 5G provides reliable safety prioritization by optimally managing both the communication channel and the prioritization of safety information through the network, while supporting a highly scalable broadcast mechanism for vehicles.

[10] *Huawei to introduce 5G networks for 2018 FIFA World Cup* (Nov. 2014), *http://www.trustedreviews.com/news/huawei-to-introduce-5g-networks-for-2018-fifa-world-cup.*

[11] *PyeongChang 2108, the ''5G Olympics''* Korea Info. Soc. (April 2016), *http://www.koreainformationsociety.com/2016/04/pyeongchang-2018-5g-olympics.html.*

[12] *Nokia, NTT DoCoMo prepare for 5G ahead of 2020 launch,* Reuters (2015), *http://www.reuters.com/article/us-telecoms-mwc-ntt-docomo-idUSKBN0LY0FD20150302*

[13] *DOCOMO Successfully Conducts 5G Trials in Actual-use Environments (2015), https://www.nttdocomo.co.jp/english/info/media\center/pr/2015/1126\00.html.*

[14] *Continental, Deutsche Telekom, Fraunhofer ESK, and Nokia Networks Showcase First Safety Applications at ''digital A9 motorway test bed''* (2015): *https://www.telekom.com/media/company/293064*

operator KT plans to conduct early 5G trials and commercialization between 2016 and 2018.[15] Clearly, the race is on and it's a crowded field.

Why Congress Should Care: The Societal and Economic Impact of IoT in Transportation

So why should policymakers care and why should they spend so much time making sure the benefits are realized in a way that enables technology in the U.S. to keep pace with global marketplace innovation? The potential impact of IoT technology to address important societal and economic challenges in the automotive and transportation sector is remarkable, compelling and exciting. The benefits that will flow from broad deployment of IoT technology in transportation is what energizes our team at Intel, and we are optimistic that enthusiasm will be contagious here in Congress.

The following is a summary of some of the many benefits of smart utilization of the IoT that have been identified for the transportation ecosystem:

Safety and Economic Savings. Improved vehicle safety is, and will remain, the consistent top priority and foundation for Intel's IoT transportation efforts. The statistics with respect to preventable automobile accidents are devastating. Every year, more than 30,000 people in the U.S. die from preventable automobile accidents,[16] and human error is the primary reason for over 90 percent of U.S. crashes.[17] An EU study found that distracted and drowsy driving were responsible for 13 percent of traffic deaths in 2014.[18] These accidents take an enormous emotional and physical toll on the driving public and their loved ones, at a cost of approximately 300,000 lives each decade in the U.S. and a cost of $190 billion each year in healthcare costs associated with accidents.[19]

Self-driving vehicles—where the vehicle senses its environment and navigates without human input—are widely expected to dramatically reduce crashes:

If only 10 percent of vehicles were self-driving:

- US traffic deaths could decrease by 1,100; and
- save almost $38 billion per year.

If 90 percent of vehicles were self-driving:

- traffic deaths could decrease by 21,700; and
- save $447 billion per year.[20]

And, when 100 percent of vehicles are self-driving, the U.S. could save $1.3 trillion per year.[21]

McKinsey similarly projects that autonomous vehicles could drastically reduce accidents, including reducing the lethality of vehicle crashes in the U.S. from second to ninth amongst accident types. They estimate that this would reduce the annual cost of roadway crashes in the U.S. from $212 billion to $22 billion—a cost savings of nearly 90 percent per year.[22]

Efficiency and Productivity. According to the United States Census Bureau, the average American commute to work is 25.4 minutes, and Americans spend 157 hours per person each year traveling on the Nation's roads and highways.[23] More-

[15] *SK Telecom announces the foundation of 5G Open Trial Specification Alliance with NTTDOCOMO, Verizon and KT* (2016): *http://www.sktelecom.com/en/press/detail.do?idx=1156*
[16] *Mortality—Motor Vehicle Traffic Deaths,* CDC, *http://www.cdc.gov/nchs/fastats/injury.htm* (site last visited June 26, 2016).
[17] *Driverless cars could reduce traffic fatalities by up to 90 percent,* says report, Science Alert ("Science Alert"), *http://www.sciencealert.com/driverless-cars-could-reduce-traffic-fatalities-by-up-to-90-says-report;* National Motor Vehicle Crash Causation Survey, U.S. Dept. of Transportation, at 25 (2008), *http://wwwnrd.nhtsa.dot.gov/pubs/811059.pdf.*
[18] Autonomous cars—game-changers for safety?, FANCI (Jan. 2016), *http://fanci-project.eu/autonomous-vehicles-changer/*
[19] Science Alert.
[20] *Preparing a Nation for Autonomous Vehicles: Opportunities, Barriers and Policy Recommendations,* Eno Center for Transportation, at 8 (Oct. 2013), *https://www.enotrans.org/wp-content/uploads/wpsc/downloadables/AV-paper.pdf.*
[21] *The 'Internet of Things' Is Now Connecting the Real Economy,* Morgan Stanley (April 2014), *http://www.technologyinvestor.com/wp-content/uploads/2014/09/internet-of-Things-2.pdf.* Specifically, $488B savings from accident avoidance, $507B productivity gain from autonomous cars, $158B fuel savings, $138B productivity gain from congestion avoidance, and $11B fuel savings from congestion avoidance.
[22] *Ten ways autonomous driving could redefine the automotive world,* McKinsey & Co., (June 2015), *http://www.mckinsey.com/industries/automotive-and-assembly/our-insights/ten-ways-autonomous-driving-could-redefine-the-automotive-world.*
[23] *Commuting in the United States 2009,* US Census Bureau (Sept. 2011), *https://www.census.gov/prod/2011pubs/acs-15.pdf*

over, the average American commuter spends 38 hours per year stuck in traffic, which collectively causes urban Americans to travel 5.5 billion more hours and purchase an extra 2.9 billion gallons of fuel; the cost to the U.S. economy of this wasted time and fuel is $121 billion per year.[24] IoT technologies like self-driving vehicles (where citizens can engage in productive activity while in transit) and more intelligent transportation infrastructure (with better traffic management) could enable a far more productive and efficient U.S. citizenry.

And for making our lives better, autonomous vehicles could free as much as 50 minutes a day for users, who will be able to spend traveling time working, relaxing, or accessing entertainment. The time saved by commuters every day might add up globally to a mind-blowing one billion hours—equivalent to twice the time it took to build the Great Pyramid of Giza. It could also create a large pool of value, potentially generating global digital-media revenues of €5 billion (over $5.5 trillion USD) per year for every additional minute people spend on the mobile Internet while in a car.[50]

Reduced traffic congestion. Traffic congestion continues to have significant impacts on urban design, land usage, and overall time usage for travelers whether for work or pleasure. This issue is in large part based on the need for vehicle parking. In a recent study, the Transportation Alternatives group found that in one Brooklyn neighborhood, 64 percent of the local cars were on local roads merely because they were searching for a parking spot.[25] Autonomous vehicles would change that by self-parking themselves in less congested areas and therefore enable city planners and developers the flexibility to reshape and improve how we use land in cities. According to Rowe,[26] one of the most profound effects of driverless vehicles would be to drastically reduce the need for parking structures and surface lots, which today take up a third of land inside cities. Some of the garages and underground structures could be converted into storage spaces for urban dwellers who live in micro units, while the unneeded surface lots would be available for commercial or residential development or green space.

New mobility options for the disabled and elderly. Nearly 15 million people across the U.S., including 6 million disabled individuals, have challenges getting the transportation they need on a daily basis.[27] These individuals often become dependent on family members or must resort to costly modes of transportation in order to travel around their communities for business, medical and social activities. Autonomous vehicles—because they do not require a human driver—can open up better transportation and mobility options for these individuals. This will both increase their individual quality of life, as well as improve our overall society. Indeed, "without access to transportation, people with disabilities will not be part of society's economic environment and will continue to be alienated from the economic mainstream, thus causing a myriad of other problems, like homelessness and institutionalization."[28]

Revenue and Growth. The automotive and transportation industries will be among the first to see immediate growth from the IoT, with global IoT revenue from the transportation sector reaching $325 billion in 2018.[29] With almost nine percent of the U.S. labor force employed in the transportation sector[30] and the U.S. spending roughly $160 billion annually on highway infrastructure (about one-fourth funded

---

[24] *The American Commuter Spends 38 Hours a Year Stuck in Traffic*, The Atlantic (Feb. 2013), *http://www.theatlantic.com/business/archive/2013/02/the-american-commuter-spends-38- hours-a-year-stuck-in-traffic/272905/*. See also *The Massive Economic Benefits Of Self-Driving Cars*, Forbes (Nov. 2014) (estimating the savings could go up to $500B/year), *http://www.forbes.com/sites/modeledbehavior/2014/11/08/the-massive-economic-benefits-of-self-driving-cars/#6bb4e79e68d9.*

[25] *How Driverless Cars Could Turn Parking Lots into City Parks*, The Atlantic (Aug. 2015), *http://www.theatlantic.com/technology/archive/2015/08/driverless-cars-robot-cabs-parking-traffic/400526/*

[26] *Imagining the Driverless City*, Urban Land Magazine (Oct. 2015), *http://urbanland.uli.org/infrastructure-transit/imagining-driverless-city/*

[27] *Transportation Difficulties Keep over Half a Million Disabled at Home*, USDOT Bureau of Transportation Statistics (2003), *http://www.rita.dot.gov/bts/sites/rita.dot.gov.bts/files/publications/special\reports\and\issue\briefs/issue\briefs/number\03/html/entire.html.*

[28] *Facts about Equity in Transportation for People with Disabilities*, The Leadership Conference on Civil and Human Rights (site last visited 6/25/16) *http://www.civilrights.org/transportation/disability/facts.html.*

[29] *Roundup of Internet of Things Forecasts And Market Estimates, 2015*, Forbes (citing IDC) (Dec. 2015), *http://www.forbes.com/sites/louiscolumbus/2015/12/27/roundup-of-internet-of-things-forecasts-and-market-estimates-2015/2/#3060c5e34a10.*

[30] *National Transportation Statistics*, U.S. Dept. of Transportation, Table 3–23 (July 2013), *http://www.rita.dot.gov/bts/sites/rita.dot.gov.bts/files/publications/na-tional\transportation\statistics/html/table\03\23.html.*

by the Federal Government)[31]—America's share of this transportation IoT revenue (and cost savings from IoT technologies) could be significant.

Fuel savings and reduction in harmful emissions. Experts such as former GM executive Larry Burns, believe driverless trucks could reduce costs in the line-haul trucking industry by 40 percent. By switching from traditional car ownership models to a shared driverless model, the costs of car ownership (based on U.S. modelling) could fall from $0.70 per mile to around $0.15 per mile—a 78 percent reduction.[32] Notably, the potential savings to the U.S. freight transportation industry alone—one of the most compelling use cases for self-driving vehicles—is estimated at $168 billion per year.[33]

First Responders. Another important benefit of mass adoption of autonomous vehicles could have a huge impact for first responders and thus the public at large. With access to driverless vehicles, emergency services could collaborate with analytics providers to improve response times and elevate the level of healthcare provided to residents while potentially lowering costs.[34]

Global Trends

But the U.S. is not alone in wanting to realize those benefits. We see a number of initiatives globally that will shape the evolution of technologies, industrial capabilities, and environmental infrastructure for autonomous vehicles to become a mainstream capability that this Committee should note as it develops its own IoT transportation vision for the U.S. A review of what is being done globally must be an essential component of your deliberations and the following may help illuminate some of the key activities that merit attention.

Country Investments in Autonomous Vehicles. The race to an autonomous vehicle world is a global one. It is important for Congress to appreciate not only the amount of funding other countries are investing in IoT transportation, but most importantly the future proof technologies in which they are investing. In short, they are largely investing in AV technologies and 5G connectivity—both of which are widely expected to achieve rapid and widespread *voluntary* adoption worldwide. If America seeks to lead the world in IoT transportation, policymakers may find interesting the countries large and strategic investments that other countries are making to drive a successful IoT transportation future and keep pace with innovation for years to come.

- *China's* search giant, Baidu, has partnered with BMW and released a semi-autonomous vehicle prototype, and has tested their technologies on highways in China. The semi-autonomous vehicle is a modified 3-Series BMW that drove an 18.6-mile route around Beijing.[35]
- *Japan* is investing in a multimillion dollar research center, called the National Innovation Complex, opened at Nagoya University last year. A key project is to develop self-driving car technology.[36]
- *Germany's* Chancellor Merkel told carmakers that they should soon be able to test self-driving vehicles on German roads by promising to remove legal barriers.[18] The stretch on the A9 autobahn—which links Munich and Berlin—will give the industry the opportunity to ''test and optimize new innovations in an adapted infrastructure that offers data connections and measuring tools.[19]
- *Sweden* is sponsoring a large-scale trial of 100 Volvo driverless cars to begin on the public roads of Gothenburg in 2017. This pilot is part of the Swedish government's vision of zero traffic fatalities, and will give insights into the technological challenges at the same time as receiving valuable feedback from real customers driving on public roads.[17]

---

[31] *Statement of Joseph Kile,* Before the U.S. Senate Cmte. on Finance, The Highway Trust Fund and Paying for Highways (May 17, 2011), *http://www.cbo.gov/sites/default/files/cbofiles/ftpdocs/121xx/doc12173/05-17-highwayfunding.pdf.*

[32] Accenture Digital at 4.

[33] *Id.* Specifically, savings from labor ($70B), fuel efficiency ($35B), productivity ($27B), and accident savings ($36B).

[34] ''*The new road to the future Realising the benefits of autonomous vehicles in Australia,''* Accenture Digital at 10 (2014) (''Accenture Digital''), *https://www.accenture.com/t00010101 T000000lwl/au-en/acnmedia/Accenture/Conversion-Assets/DotCom/Documents/Local/en-gb/PDF13/Accenture-Realising-Benefits-Autonomous-Vehicles-Australia.pdf*

[35] *China's roadmap to self-driving cars,* Fortune (April 2016), *http://fortune.com/2016/04/23/china-self-driving-cars/?iid=sr-link2; Inside China's Plan to Beat America to the Self-Driving Car,* Wired (June 2016), *https://www.wired.com/2016/06/chinas-plan-first-country-self-driving-cars/*

[36] *Scania to test Ericsson 5G for V2X applications,* Safe Car News (May 2016), *http://safecarnews.com/scania-to-test-ericsson-5g-for-v2x-applications-ma7311/*

- *Korea.* The Korean government has pledged 145.5 billion won ($127.7 million USD) to develop key technologies for self-driving cars in hopes of beating out global competitors, including leading IT companies, beginning in 2017.[37]
- *The UK* announced £20 million (over $27 million USD) of its £100 million Intelligent Mobility Fund will be invested in autonomous vehicle advancement, including current trials to test driverless cars on the streets of Bristol, Coventry and Milton Keynes, and Greenwich, and developing autonomous shuttles to carry visually-impaired passengers using advanced sensors and control systems.[38]

A review of what the auto industry has undertaken to date also is vital for your strategic planning. Again, we see advancements occurring worldwide:

Status of Autonomous Vehicles. Both traditional automakers and new automotive innovators are racing to deliver a self-driving vehicle world—largely predicting mainstream autonomous vehicles on market by or before 2020.[39]

Highly Autonomous Cars on Market Today

- *2015 Infiniti Q50S:* Intelligent Cruise Control, Predictive Forward Collision Warning, Forward Emergency Braking, Lane Departure Warning/Prevention, Active Lane Control
- *2015 Mercedes-Benz S65 AMG Coupe:* Distronic Plus with Steering Assist, Adaptive Brake Technology, Active Lane-Keeping Assist
- *2016 Tesla Model S P85D/P90D:* Autopilot, Autosteer, Auto Lane Change, Autopark, Traffic-Aware Cruise Control
- *2016 Volvo XC90 T6/T8 Hybrid:* Intellisafe Autopilot
- *2016 Honda Civic:* Semi-autonomous ADAS
- *2016 BMW 750i xDrive:* Driver Assistance Plus, Active Driving Assistant Plus

Near-Term Highly Autonomous Prototypes

- *Lexus GS 450h:* Intelligent Safety Concept
- *Faraday Future FFZERO1 EV Concept:* Self-driving, almost fully autonomous
- *Audi RS7:* Driving Concept Car
- *Acura RLX Sedan:* Self-Driving Prototype

Fully Autonomous Cars 2017–2021

- *Audi* expects its A8 to be capable of fully autonomous driving next year in 2017.[40]
- *Volvo* pledged no accidents in its cars by 2020 due to autonomous technology[41] and announced a 100-car public trial with Swedish authorities where *members of public* will be behind wheel.[42]
- *Google* plans to have its driverless cars on the market no later than 2018.[43]
- *Tesla* Founder expects first fully autonomous Tesla vehicles by 2018.[44]

[37] *Gov't pledges 145.5 billion won for self-driving technology,* Korea Joon Gang Daily (April 2016), *http://koreajoongangdaily.joins.com/news/article/Article.aspx?aid=3018172*

[38] *Driverless car technology receives £20 million boost* (Feb. 2016), *https://www.gov.uk/government/news/driverless-cars-technology-receives-20-million-boost; Driverless cars to be tested on UK motorways in 2017,* Wired.uk (March 2016) *http://www.wired.co.uk/article/budget-support-driverless-car-trials-uk-motorways-2017.*

[39] *Driverless car market: Gearing up to save lives, reduce costs, resource consumption* (''Self-Driving Forecast''), *http://www.driverless-future.com/?pageid=384* (site last visited 6/22/16).

[40] *Next-gen Audi A8 drives better than you,* Motoring (Oct. 2014), *http://www.motoring.com.au/next-gen-audi-a8-drives-better-than-you-46963/.*

[41] *Volvo's 2020 pledge: No one will die in our cars,* CS Monitor/AP (Jan. 2016), *http://www.csmonitor.com/Technology/2016/0121/Volvo-s-2020-pledge-No-one-will-die-in-our-cars*

[42] *Volvo to test autonomous cars with ordinary drivers on public roads by 2017,* The Guardian (Feb. 2015), *https://www.theguardian.com/technology/2015/feb/24/volvo-test-autonomous-cars-ordinary-drivers-public-roads-by-2017*

[43] *Sergey Brin on driverless car future,* Driverless Car Market Watch (Oct. 2012), *http://www.driverless-future.com/?p=323*

[44] *Elon Musk Says Tesla Vehicles Will Drive Themselves in Two Years,* Fortune (Dec. 2015), *http://fortune.com/2015/12/21/elon-musk-interview/*

- *Baidu* expects a large number of self-driving cars on the road by 2019, with mass-production in full swing by 2021.[45]
- *Volkswagen* expects the first self-driving cars to appear on the market by 2019.[46]
- *Ford* CEO expects to have self-driving cars by 2020.[47] Similarly, *Changan* (Ford's partner in China) said a self-driving model should be on the market in 2–3 years, with the automaker spending 5 billion yuan ($773 million USD) to further the technology by 2020.[48]
- *Daimler,* the maker of Mercedes Benz, plans to have its driverless trucks ready by 2020.[49] *Uber* placed an order for 100,000 Mercedes self-driving sedans for its ride-sharing service by 2020.[50]
- *Nissan* will make fully autonomous vehicles available to the consumer by 2020.[51]
- *Toyota,* the maker of Lexus, plans to bring its first models capable of autonomous highway driving to the market by 2020.[52]
- *GM* predicts that most industry participants now think that self-driving cars will be on the road by 2020 or sooner.[53]
- *BMW* CEO Harald Krueger said that BMW will launch a self-driving electric vehicle, the BMW iNext, in 2021.[54]

IoT Automotive Technologies

There also is good reason to review the fact that, within the transportation sector, there are two distinct yet often conflated technologies: the "connected car" and the "autonomous vehicle" (self-driving car). The first—with the rapid evolution to 5G cellular technology—may precede the second, but provides a great example of how technologies and capabilities rapidly advanced once the foundational capability for connecting cars was established. The same will likely hold true for autonomous vehicles once the foundational technologies are in place.

Connected car. The connected car has existed for many years with increasingly sophisticated capabilities. From the initial built-in cellular connectivity, the capabilities today include real-time navigation and traffic updates as well as Internet web connectivity for on-board apps. In most countries, "connected car" is a broad term indicating that the vehicle is equipped with one or more technologies that enable Internet access—most often via a wireless network using advanced cellular (like 4G/LTE, 5G) and/or Wi-Fi technologies. A "connected car" shares Internet access with other devices both inside as well as outside the vehicle, enabling passengers to access features including in-car entertainment, smartphone apps, navigation, roadside service and car diagnostics. (By contrast, USDOT tends to narrowly use the term "connected vehicle" to refer only to a vehicle with the agency's preferred V2V safety

[45] *China's Baidu Could Beat Google to Self-Driving Car with BMW,* The Guardian (June 2015), https://www.theguardian.com/technology/2015/jun/10/baidu-could-beat-google-self-driving-car-bmw.

[46] Self-Driving Forecast; see also *Die Zukunft nach dem Abgas-Skandal,* Focus Magazine (April 2016), http://www.focus.de/finanzen/news/wirtschaft-und-geld-die-zukunft-nach-dem-abgas-skandal\id\5457885.html

[47] *Ford's self-driving cars likely around 2020,* USA Today (Jan. 2016), http://www.usatoday.com/story/tech/2016/01/05/ford-reaffirms-multi-pronged-auto-tech-approaches/78301192/

[48] *Inside China's Plan to Beat America to the Self-Driving Car,* Wired (June 2016), https://www.wired.com/2016/06/chinas-plan-first-country-self-driving-cars/

[49] *Daimler tests autonomous big-rig convoy on public roads,* Road & Track (March 2016), http://www.roadandtrack.com/new-cars/car-technology/news/a28548/daimler-tests-autono-mous-big-rig-convoy-on/

[50] *After considering Tesla, Uber reportedly placed an order with Mercedes for 100,000 self-driving cars,* Electrek (March 2016), http://electrek.co/2016/03/18/uber-order-mercedes-100000-autonomous-cars/.

[51] *Nissan's autonomous drive car,* Nissan USA (March 2014), http://www.nissanusa.com/blog/autonomous-drive-car

[52] *Toyota to launch first driverless car in 2020,* Wired UK (Oct 2015), http://www.wired.co.uk/article/toyota-highway-teammate-driverless-car-tokyo

[53] *GM executive credits Silicon Valley for accelerating development of self-driving cars,* WSJ (May 2016), http://www.wsj.com/articles/gm-executive-credits-silicon-valley-for-accelerating-development-of-self-driving-cars-1462910491

[54] *BMW will launch the electric and autonomous iNext in 2021, new i8 in 2018 and not much in-between,* Elektrek (May 2016), http://electrek.co/2016/05/12/bmw-electric-autonomous-inext-2021/

technology: Dedicated Short Range Communications or DSRC in the 5.9 GHz[55] spectrum band.) These solutions will rapidly evolve to use two-way Internet connectivity to communicate with not only other vehicles V2V but also infrastructure (V2I) and other "things" (V2X).

While this hearing is not intended to delve into spectrum policy, we would note that U.S. policymakers will ultimately need to address the path for various technologies. For example, nearly all studies projecting future marketplace penetration of connected vehicles are using the broader definition to reflect the projected pervasiveness of advanced cellular (5G), Wi-Fi, Bluetooth and satellite communications—not DSRC.[56] For example, Gartner predicts that by 2020, there will be a quarter billion connected vehicles on the road.[57] This connected car market is projected to generate new services revenue from connected cars at approximately $40 billion annually by 2020.[58]

With 4G LTE now deployed in nearly every major market, the rapid evolution and market demand for cellular technologies like LTE-Advanced (LTE–A) and 5th generation cellular (5G), along with next generation Wi-Fi and Bluetooth, are driving this connected car innovation. These cellular technologies are the product of a competitive marketplace with significant and constantly evolving industry R&D, strong industry investment in wide-scale deployment, and very rapid and high marketplace adoption. If the U.S. seeks to capture a strong portion of this $40 billion per year connected car services market, it is imperative that the Nation's policies and resources support public and private investment in these advanced cellular technologies, including testbeds for cellular V2V safety critical communications and real-time safety messaging and collision avoidance.

Autonomous vehicle (AV). As its name implies, the self-driving vehicle is capable of operating without a driver. It uses a complex array of tools to help it navigate real world conditions of day-to-day driving. For example, the Google self-driving car uses a mix of radar, LIDAR (measures distances by illuminating a target with laser light), HD cameras, advanced GPS and HD mapping to sense its environment and surroundings. *There is no DSRC connectivity in the Google car;* although it is widely expected that 5G connectivity will be added to many self-driving cars.

Autonomous cars also have the ability to make driving decisions based on complex analysis of data from these sensing elements. Self-driving cars also may have (but need not) Internet connectivity; for example, they may use 4G or 5G cellular communications as secondary source of information for V2V real-time collision avoidance, in addition to the on-board sensor-based systems which provide their primary source of data. In short, the vehicle is increasingly becoming smarter, more complex, processing more data and effectively becoming a "data center on wheels." Intel has been leading the industry in data center technology for decades and appreciates the importance of secure, efficient and reliable computing.

There are a number of technologies that are essential to the evolution of these solutions. Sensors have been and will continue to evolve rapidly. As noted, cameras and LIDAR as well as radar and ultrasound are used to help the car "see" what's around it. These sensors are being refined to be more purpose built for this specific application. Data from these sensors must then be integrated (sometimes called sensor fusion) at a first order to provide very fast initial indications of the environment. That data is then fed into very high performance computing platforms that can then process the data and make decisions about the control of the vehicle. The processing today is largely done according to algorithms that have been refined based on environmental understanding and knowledge of driving decisions. Going forward though, these decisions will be made using sophisticated "machine learning" (ML) and "deep learning" (DL) technologies like vision-based object recognition which allows the vehicle to 'see' the objects in the environment around it—pedestrians, other cars, road signs, etc. These systems will gather data from vehicles on an on-going basis (called "scoring), send that data to the datacenter or cloud, continuously "learn" from what is happening from the fleet of vehicles on the road (called "training"), improve the driving model, and then send the improved model back down to the fleet. These systems must become well integrated end-to-end solutions that have persistent connectivity to the datacenter, and are able to evolve rapidly to meet the needs of more and more sophisticated transportation solutions.

---

[55] 5.9 GHz and 5G are entirely different things. 5.9 GHz is the embattled *spectrum band* in which DSRC technology would operate. Whereas 5G is a *cellular technology* (that operates in non-5.9 GHz spectrum bands).

[56] *See, e.g.,* Connected Car Report, Gartner (2015), *http://www.gartner.com/newsroom/id/2970017.*

[57] *Id.*

[58] *Id.*

In the last few years, there has been a remarkable acceleration in autonomous vehicle investment, innovation and testing around the world. Discussions of IoT innovations and autonomous vehicles have quickly migrated from niche engineering and auto industry websites to mainstream publications. Seemingly from out of the blue, the term "self-driving car" has entered into our everyday lexicon—with U.S. and global consumers of all ages *demanding* (and even *expecting*) sensor-based collision avoidance technologies like predictive collision warning, automatic breaking, parking assist and active lane control when purchasing new cars. A recent study by The Harford and MIT AgeLab found that, like younger generations, 76 percent of drivers age 50–69 purposefully seek out high-tech autonomous vehicle safety features.[59]

Moreover, the pace of autonomous vehicle investments and announcements around the globe have further accelerated in just the last 6 months. Over this time period, Intel has seen ship dates from our auto industry customers "pull in" (move up) by as much as 5 years, as these companies have come to fully realize that they must accelerate their technology innovation time-to-market or be left behind. Indeed, these self-driving technologies—which seemed like a far off "Jetsons" fantasy just five years ago—seem just around the corner today.

In order to turn this autonomous vision into a reality, the auto industry and transportation providers of the future must harness rapidly evolving technologies, collaborate with new partners like the high-tech industry, and embrace disruptive opportunities to innovate. This autonomous driving future will only continue to accelerate as technology advancements and the competitive marketplace further enable automakers to go to market with new autonomous vehicle innovations in an increasingly expedited manner to deliver on the vision of a zero accidents future.

Policy Recommendations for a National IoT Transportation Strategy

Countries around the world are moving aggressively ahead on establishing national plans and blueprints with time-bound measurable goals, investing substantial funding in AV and 5G cellular V2V safety research and deployments, and launching PPPs to jumpstart these opportunities to quickly enable scale. As these other countries have recognized, a forward-looking IoT transportation strategy that will *keep pace with global innovation* is essential. It is critical for U.S. policymakers to enable a vibrant and state-of-the-art transportation system to ensure the Nation's global competitiveness and economic stability in the 21st century. By adopting and implementing a National IoT Transportation Strategy for autonomous vehicles and 5G-enabled connected cars, the U.S. will be poised to secure a worldwide leadership position in this next evolution of transportation.

As a part of our larger U.S. National IoT Strategy (that would be developed pursuant to the new USDOC/NTIA IoT green paper process and the pending bipartisan DIGIT Act),[60] Intel recommends that the following principles drive our National IoT Transportation Strategy:

Prioritize Safety and Security. Enhanced safety is vital to the success of America's IoT transportation future. Safety means (i) reducing the number and severity of crashes and (ii) protecting consumers and businesses from security breaches of the vast amount of data generated by their vehicles. With respect to crashes, self-driving vehicles will remove the risk of human error, and thus are widely expected to reduce U.S. traffic deaths by tens of thousands per year, as discussed in detail above. With respect to security, future vehicles will generate a tremendous amount of "data exhaust" as they seamlessly connect to each other, infrastructure and consumer electronic devices and enable autonomous tasks.[61] For example, a self-driving car could generate as much as two petabytes of data per year.[62]

Security. Intel values security first and foremost. We believe that security is the foundation of IoT transportation and it is fundamental to Intel's roadmap planning. Our hardware and software are *being designed from the beginning to be secure.* This is important for trusted data exchange in the IoT, as data generated by devices (including vehicles) and infrastructure must be able to be shared among the cloud, the

[59] *Looking Forward: Vehicle Technology Preferences Among Mature Drivers,* The Hartford Center for Mature Market Excellence® and MIT AgeLab (2016), *http://extramile.thehartford.com/auto/vehicle-technology-preferences-mature-drivers.*

[60] *Developing Innovation and Growing the Internet of Things Act* (2016), *https://www.fischer.senate.gov/public/\cache/files/03de7771-088b-45ac-8552-f82ddc0aa480/digit-2016\final-bill-for-filing.pdf.*

[61] The Future of Intelligent Transportation: *http://www.intel.com/content/www/us/en/automotive/experiencing-future-intelligent-transportation-video.html*

[62] *A Self-Driving Car Will Create 1 GB of Data per Second,* SmartData Collective (July 2013) ("Smart Data"), *http://www.smartdatacollective.com/bigdatastartups/135291/self-driving-cars-will-create-2-petabytes-data-what-are-big-data-opportunitie.*

network, and intelligent devices for analysis. This enables users to aggregate, filter and share data from the edge of the network all the way to the cloud with robust protection. Data also must be accurate to be beneficial. Intel prioritizes the security, accuracy, privacy and integrity of data in all market sectors, and especially in the industrial (including transportation) domain where the safeguarding of critical infrastructure can be vital to economic and social stability.

Intel appreciates that we must deliver and evoke consumer and industry trust through these hardened security solutions to motivate adoption and participation in the IoT marketplace. We believe it is critical to integrate security into the hardware *and* software, from the smallest microcontroller (MCU) at the edge of the network to the most advanced server central processing unit (CPU) in the cloud and all gateways[63] and devices in between. These hardware-and software-level security capabilities create redundancies which prevent intrusions and enable a robust, secure, trusted IoT end-to-end solution.

Hardware. Intel's hardware provides transistor-level security *on the actual compute device itself.* By integrating security into the device itself from the outset (rather than layering it on top at a latter point in the design cycle with other, less secure external features), Intel's IoT solutions enable our customers to know the exact unique identity of every device on their network. This technology also has the capability for encrypting that unique identity to provide anonymity properties in addition to hardware enforced integrity. Because each compute device can have an immutable identification to enable secure provisioning, a non-approved device will not be allowed to access the network. The MCU or CPU itself will provide the "baked in" (irremovable, non-changeable) identity of the device, making the level of security significantly more robust.

On top of this immutable device identification, Intel's IoT solutions employ advanced hardware level security capabilities such as "whitelisting," which prevents harmful applications like viruses, control agents, and malware from ever being activated on the device. What this means is that, if the CPU ever "sees" an application that is not on its known good list ("whitelist") try to run on the device, it will automatically lock out that device and not allow it turn on. At other layers in IoT solutions, Intel also uses another advanced hardware security capability called "blacklisting," which blocks a defined list of known malware from entering the device and the network.

Software. In addition to the advanced hardware security capabilities in Intel's IoT solutions, Intel Security (formerly McAfee) integrates advanced security capabilities that provide robust software-level protection. This means that the software is continually monitoring the activity of its networked devices-and looking for any abnormalities or possible threats. If the monitoring software identifies a threat, it proactively notifies users and/or automatically quarantines any devices on the network that could be at risk. By employing this combination of transistor-level security, along with advanced hardware and software level security, from devices on the edge of the network all the way to the data centers in the cloud, Intel protects IoT assets and information in ways few others can. We know that security is critical to protect the integrity of IoT solutions, so we will design it in from the outset.

We also must account for the distinct security challenges of autonomous and connected features, harnessing appropriate technical and policy strategies to mitigate risks and enable a safe, secure vehicle that evokes trust from drivers and passengers on U.S. highways. Autonomous vehicle solutions use local sensors and "intelligence" to provide a highly secure, self-contained, robust source of data. By contrast, a vehicle's "connected" features exchange data between two "things"—with the Internet, other cars, and infrastructure—potentially making this threat landscape more vulnerable. This is one of many reasons why it is exceedingly important that we look to advanced cellular technologies like today's 4G and the soon-to-arrive 5G for applications like V2V safety critical communications (vs. a system with multiple *known* vulnerabilities like USDOT's proposed DSRC Security Credential Management System).[64]

Encourage Innovation and Competition. Self-driving vehicle technology, connected cars, "smart" fleet management and intelligent transportation infrastructure have

---

[63] A gateway is a node on a network that serves as an entrance to another network.

[64] SCMS relies on sporadic connection between the vehicle and infrastructure to validate and revoke certificates initiated by the Certifying Authority. This sporadic connection can cause large delays in revoking security certificates and can erroneously permit non-secure and unauthenticated messages to be transmitted to/among vehicles. By contrast, cellular networks use mechanisms to robustly protect vehicles from cybersecurity incidents; persistent cellular connections help accelerate certificate update, distribution, and revocation, making certificate management much more effective, secure and reliable.

enormous potential to improve driving safety, mobility, energy use, and transportation efficiency—paving the way for U.S. smart cities of tomorrow. Innovation and market competition—in tandem with light-touch, adaptive, technology neutral, performance-based regulation—must drive our Nation's policy framework and guidelines to enable the U.S. to lead the world in the automotive and transportation sector of the future.

As we know, regulation of technology, however well intended, will always lag marketplace innovation and often thwart innovation. This can be true even in areas of extreme importance such as building secure networks and technologies. In order to position the U.S. to lead the rest of the world in the globally competitive IoT transportation future, USDOT R&D funding should help enable and accelerate industry-driven investment. The agency should never seek to choose, mandate or direct the technologies which U.S. companies develop or in which they invest, nor should it put its thumb on the scale or try to drive a specific market outcome. Public policies that encourage innovation, competition, and market-driven investment are critical to enable U.S. leadership in IoT technologies like connected cars and self-driving vehicles to reach their full potential, realize maximum economic and safety benefits, and become widely available in a timely and globally competitive manner.

Promote technology neutrality. Pursuant to the *FAST Act* [65] Joint Explanatory Statement: [66] ''The *FAST Act* ensures that [USDOT] programs are implemented and Intelligent Transportation Systems are deployed in a technology neutral manner. The Act promotes technology neutral policies that accelerate vehicle and transportation safety research, development and deployment by promoting innovation and competitive market-based outcomes, while using Federal funds efficiently and leveraging private sector investment across the automotive, transportation and technology sectors.'' As drafted by bicameral and bipartisan Members of Congress, this statement should serve as a constant guiding principle; it is critical that USDOT drive technology-neutral policies based on competitive market-based outcomes to ensure U.S. consumers benefit from the life-saving capabilities of the most advanced technologies, which *stay apace with technology evolution* for decades to come.

It is imperative that the U.S. align our future transportation strategy with the realities and direction of the worldwide open, competitive marketplace and the areas of largest global investment. We must architect and adopt a leading-edge, future-proof strategy that invests primarily in AVs (self-driving cars) and 5G cellular technology starting with V2V real-time collision avoidance applications. However, USDOT is not promoting—or even seriously researching—advanced cellular technologies like 5G for V2V safety critical applications, which many industry experts believe will be the leading global V2V safety technology.[67] For the U.S. to stay apace our global competitors, Congress should direct USDOT to undertake a meaningful, technology-neutral cost-benefit analysis vs. DSRC [68] to ensure that U.S. consumers are poised to reap the benefits of the best V2V safety technology(ies) that will *evolve at the pace of marketplace innovation*—and enable U.S. IoT transportation leadership now and in the future.

Most of the world is developing and testing AVs and 5G connectivity for real-time collision avoidance *independent of DSRC* (if they are testing DSRC at all). Let the technologies' capabilities determine marketplace winners and losers, rather than force industry investment in a technology (DSRC) chosen in 1999 before mobile broadband even existed—and that will put the U.S. behind other countries. Seventeen years later, we should be investing in the future (aligned with the greater global marketplace), rather than forcing U.S. investment in an old technology. If we invest the time now to do broader technology R&D and transition to a more future-proof strategy, policymakers will be ensuring that U.S. consumers have the benefit of the best collision avoidance technolology(ies) that *will evolve at the pace of inno-*

---

[65] *H.R. 22, Fixing America's Surface Transportation Act* (2015), *https://www.congress.gov/114/bills/hr22/BILLS-114hr22enr.pdf.*

[66] Joint Explanatory Statement of the Committee of the Conference at 10 (2015), *http://transportation.house.gov/uploadedfiles/joint\explanatory\statement.pdf.*

[67] *See, e.g.,* DSRC Confronts a Battle for relevance at ITS World Congress (2014): *https://www.strategyanalytics.com/access-services/automotive/powertrain-body-chassis-and-safety/reports/report-detail/dsrc-confronts-a-battle-for-relevance-at-its-world-congress?Related#.Vwgur\krJD8*

[68] It is critical that the Nation's limited funding be invested in 5G and AVs *independent of* DSRC, as AVs and 5G connectivity operate independently of (and without need for) DSRC. Yet, USDOT investment in AVs and cellular to date primarily have encouraged a DSRC aspect to the test bed or project. Despite many comments by high-tech industry advocating advanced cellular/5G for V2V safety and questioning a DSRC mandate in the agency's 2014 V2V ANPRM, USDOT still has not funded any advanced cellular testbeds for V2V safety communications that would enable a head-to-head comparison with DSRC.

vation. Without this, we risk thwarting U.S. global leadership and, more importantly, the potential to save more American lives.

DSRC has been slow to develop (in testing phase for nearly two decades) and is not poised to evolve at the pace of innovation because the marketplace is unlikely to see the global industry support or voluntary widespread market demand that would enable economies of scale. Also, unlike 5G, which industry is evolving from existing 4G networks and infrastructure, DSRC will require entirely new infrastructure at massive taxpayer expense for years to come; the cost of building and deploying new infrastructure for DSRC and covering all necessary rural and urban areas is estimated to be approximately $3,000/mile.[69] For these reasons, innovations like next generation cellular 5G are developed, tested, built out and commercialized at a far faster pace than DSRC—and will continue to evolve on pace with innovation. In the end, the losers will be U.S. consumers deprived of the best cellular V2V safety technologies that evolve on pace with a competitive marketplace.

Encourage Open Platforms. Open IoT technology platforms are critical to the ability of U.S. companies to compete globally because they ensure cross-industry support and agreement. Open platforms allow multiple manufacturers to ''plug in'' their technologies, while proprietary platforms only allow use of a single manufacturer's proprietary technology. This encourages developers to create solutions that span from car to cloud in a simple way. Government should encourage industry to collaborate on open platforms for autonomous and connected vehicles.

Open platforms are necessary to accelerate and maximize innovation across the increasingly broadening automotive and transportation industries and enable economies of scale. For example, Intel is widely deploying ''state of the art'' autonomous reference platforms that are open, standards-based and scalable to support safe and secure computing both in the vehicle and the connected data center. This enables other stakeholders and innovators to contribute core technology including platform software, machine learning algorithms and data collected from vehicle sensors to enable a safe and secure driving experience.

Support Open Standards and Consortia Efforts. Global standards and consortia efforts are critical to maintain the long term viability of technology advancements. They enable a commercialization path that is scalable, interoperable and reusable across a variety of use case deployments, vendors and sectors. Accordingly, a certain level of standardization and interoperability is vital to the successful commercialization of self-driving vehicles, connected cars, ''smart'' fleet management and the intelligent transportation ecosystem. Industry-led voluntary global standards can accelerate adoption, drive competition, and enable cost-effective introduction of new technologies, while providing a clearer technology evolution path that stimulates investment.

Industry is in the best position to lead development of technological standards and solutions to address global transportation ecosystem opportunities and challenges to enable self-driving vehicles, connected vehicles, ''smart'' fleet management and intelligent transportation systems. *Policymakers should refrain from mandating specific technologies, standards, or protocols* and, instead, let the marketplace determine technology winners and losers. Government should encourage industry to collaborate in global, open-participation standardization efforts to develop technological best practices and standards, and it should participate in the development of standards where there is a government interest and encourage the use of commercially available solutions to enable the benefits of these new technologies to become reality sooner.

Invest in Public-Private Partnerships. The tech industry is critical to the future of U.S. transportation policy dialogue. A vehicle is an increasingly complex data center on wheels, requiring evermore high-powered processors and Internet connectivity—with self-driving cars expected to process at 1 GB of data per second.[70] As part of a National IoT Transportation Strategy, policymakers should encourage Public-Private Partnerships (PPPs) to launch and scale globally competitive transportation test beds. These testbeds are necessary to accelerate deployment of technologies such as 5G which is critical to U.S. leadership in V2V safety-critical and V2X communications and machine learning which is critical to autonomous driving.

Government and industry collaboration can be one of our Nation's best assets to accelerate the adoption of world-class transportation systems. Viable PPPs between government and the auto and tech industries must entail logical investments for both government and industry, as well as ensure scalability of automotive innovations and sustainability of transportation infrastructure in the long term. Using

---

[69] *5G–PPP Automotive White Paper* (Oct. 2015).
[70] Smart Data.

public and private resources to facilitate U.S. research leadership, and governance for in 5G connectivity and autonomous driving, while leveraging existing industry standards and investments, will accelerate our future toward self-driving vehicles, connected cars, ''smart'' fleet management, and intelligent transportation infrastructure.

Intel recommends that policymakers encourage PPPs in the following areas that are critical to the success of safe and secure autonomous and connected vehicles:

- *Trusted Data and Secure Compute*—Fully autonomous driving will require the processing capabilities of a ''mini data center on wheels.'' A self-driving car will require up to 40 Teraflops of computer graphics processing speed, which is the equivalent to 20 HD TVs inside each vehicle. Compare: A Play Station 4 uses only 1.84 Teraflops. Along with this enormous computing power, every data exchange to and from the vehicle must be trusted, safe and secure. As discussed above, powerful computing with integrated security is Intel's core competency, and what our data center customers have required for decades.

- *5G Connectivity*—As discussed at the outset, soon-to-be launched 5G—boasts superior key performance indicators for vehicle connectivity use cases, especially V2V safety-critical applications. To align the Industry, Intel is driving standards workgroups in 3GPP and the Wi-Fi Alliance to influence new standards, converge protocols and demonstrate functionally safe and secure safety-critical use cases. Intel and our partners around the world in the academic, auto and technology industries are working collaboratively to drive robust, open, secure and scalable 5G standards for V2V safety-critical communications.

- *Security as a Foundation*—Intel has long touted security as a foundation for the IoT. Securing connected vehicles and the supporting infrastructure is foundational to keeping passengers safe and secure and requires an end-to-end system (vehicle to cloud) approach. Not only must every vehicle be safeguarded against cyber threats, but every device connected to the vehicle and the personal information available via these devices, must also be kept private as it moves between the vehicle, connected devices, connected infrastructure, and the cloud. Intel formed the Automotive Security Review Board[71] to help align the tech and automotive industries and cybersecurity experts on guidelines and best practices to make vehicles secure.

- *Machine Learning*—The fully autonomous vehicle must become the ultimate learning machine. It will be relied upon to make smarter and safer decisions than even the most skilled human driver. Intel has been investing in companies with expertise in functional safety[72] and doing foundational research in Deep Learning for many years and is working to ensure that our products both in the vehicle and in the data center are capable of bringing the intelligence needed for the vehicle to sense and adapt.

- *Open, Standards-Based Platforms*—Intel is working with fellow tech and auto industry leaders to define industry standards to accelerate autonomous driving deployments and create economies of scale that enable rapid marketplace adoption. This will enable industry leaders to contribute core technology including platform software, machine learning algorithms and data collected from vehicle sensors to enable a safe and secure driving experience.

Conclusion

Intel appreciates the opportunity to share our perspective on the enormous opportunity of the IoT in the transportation sector. We look forward to working with this Committee and other policymakers to develop a strategy for U.S. leadership in the next evolution of transportation—one that is poised to evolve at the pace of innovation.

Senator FISCHER. Thank you very much.

Next, we have Dr. Robert Edelstein, Senior Vice President of AECOM. Welcome.

---

[71] *Intel commits to mitigating automotive cyber security risks*, Intel Corp. (Sept. 2015), *https:// newsroom.intel.com/news-releases/intel-commits-to-mitigating-automotive-cybersecurity-risks/*.

[72] *Intel Acquires Yogitech to Strengthen its Internet of Things Group*, Venture Capital Post (April 2016), *http://www.vcpost.com/articles/119131/20160407/intel-yogitech-altera-corp-autonomous-vehicles.htm*

STATEMENT OF DR. ROBERT EDELSTEIN, SENIOR VICE PRESIDENT, ITS PRACTICE LEAD, AECOM

Dr. EDELSTEIN. Chairman Fischer, Ranking Member Booker, members of the Subcommittee, on behalf of AECOM, I would like to thank you for the opportunity to testify on the advancement of new technologies to enhance our transportation and infrastructure across the country.

AECOM is a Fortune 500 firm where we integrate design, build, operations, maintenance, as well as finance of infrastructure programs. According to Engineering News-Record, we ranked number one in transportation as well as other market sectors.

Over the years, we have seen transportation management centers, or TMCs, evolve from becoming single-dimensional to multi-dimensional, multimodal, and multijurisdictional. We look at the next wave as incorporating predictive algorithms and automated decision support systems so we can stay ahead of congestion rather than reacting to it.

AECOM is a global leader in TMCs. Our forte is really in the area of operations where we operate at over 40 facilities throughout the United States. In Florida and California, we developed dynamic pricing software to support the managed lane systems. In Virginia, we've operated the reversible roadway systems. In New Jersey, we've worked with IBM in developing the next generation of advanced traffic management systems software, positioning themselves to incorporate the predictive algorithms and decision support systems in the future. In Michigan, we operate four TMCs, and that is really the hotbed of all connected vehicle testbeds as well as research. As well as Missouri, where we are operating the gateway TMC, which will be accommodating the new innovations of the Road to Tomorrow program in the near future.

The pace of change in this area really creates a critical need for extensive technology partnerships. Strong and adaptive technology partnerships allow communities to build upon the lessons learned from previous efforts across the country.

AECOM has collaborated with firms like Xerox, where we developed the dynamic pricing software, with IBM working on smart city projects over in India, as well as work that we have done in New Jersey. Next month, we were selected and will be starting work with the Colorado Department of Transportation on the RoadX program. We've also been supporting the Missouri DOT on their Road to Tomorrow program and coming up with new technology partnerships and new innovations.

The Internet of Things provides endless opportunities for TMCs to grow. As no one owns the Internet, nor the controls or the information that is transmitted across it, the same can be said about the Internet of Things. There are about 75 million servers that operate the global Internet. There are 1.2 billion cars on roadway systems throughout the world, more than 20 percent here in the United States. But cars are inefficient. They are parked 95 percent of the time. Our transportation systems outside the peak hours and the middays are significantly underutilized.

So there is a reason why leading global Internet companies are looking at connected and autonomous vehicles as they understand the issues are similar to the decentralization that created the Internet many decades ago.

IoT approaches will allow people and cargo to be transported more efficiently across multimodal transportation networks at designated pickup and drop-off times. This will enable the balancing of transportation supply and demand in real-time and allow the user, the end-user, to optimize their trips based on what's right for them in terms of the modes that they use, the schedules, and the routes.

In recent years, there have been several innovations that have been incorporated into our transportation systems—smart roadways, data management systems, integrated corridor management, and now most of the attention is being focused in on the connected and autonomous vehicles.

I would like to leave you with my vision of the future for the TMC of the future, at least in my perspective. The TMC of the present continues to focus in on traffic operations and safety, and rightfully so, while the TMC of the future will start accommodating these next-generation ITS strategies—managed lanes, active traffic management, et cetera.

The Internet of Things will start to include both transportation and nontransportation functions together. While this integration may be virtual or it may be a collocation of operations staff, and there are some advantages and disadvantages to both approaches, the integration has the potential to open up new areas to apply the IoT and big data to operate our systems more efficiently, so I would ask that you consider the TMC of the future when we start building our Smart Cities.

And my testimony that I'm submitting for the record has included a number of policy recommendations that I would like you to consider as you deal with these issues in the future. So on behalf of AECOM, I would like to thank you for receiving my testimony. I look forward to your questions.

[The prepared statement of Dr. Edelstein follows:]

PREPARED STATEMENT OF DR. ROBERT EDELSTEIN, SENIOR VICE PRESIDENT, ITS PRACTICE LEAD, AECOM

Chairman Fischer, Ranking Member Booker, and members of the Subcommittee, on behalf of AECOM, I thank you for this opportunity to testify on the advancement of new technologies to enhance infrastructure and transportation across the country. Whether we are discussing the so-called ''Internet of Things'' (IoT) in transportation and infrastructure, or more broadly, the application of technology, and the utilization and analysis of data to evaluate, manage and improve system performance, there is much being accomplished in this area.

My name is Robert Edelstein, and I am a Senior Vice President and Intelligent Transportation Systems (ITS) Practice Leader for AECOM.

When I joined AECOM in 1978, my focus was largely on the planning, design and construction of transportation facilities including roadways, transit systems, airports, seaports, and multimodal transportation centers. This focus has transitioned to making these infrastructure projects more efficient in terms of operational integration. This is now facilitated through the advent IoT and big data applications.

About AECOM

AECOM is a premier, fully integrated professional and technical services firm positioned to design, build, finance, operate and maintain infrastructure assets around the world for public and private sector clients. We have nearly 92,000 employees—including architects, engineers, designers, planners, scientists and management and construction services professionals—serving clients in over 150 countries around the world. AECOM is ranked—for the seventh consecutive year—as the #1 engineering design firm by revenue in Engineering News-Record magazine's annual industry rankings, and has been recognized by Fortune magazine as a World's Most Admired Company. The firm is a leader in all of the key markets that it serves, including transportation, facilities, environmental, energy, oil and gas, water, high-rise buildings and government. AECOM provides a blend of global reach, local knowledge, innovation and technical excellence in delivering customized and creative solutions that meet the needs of clients' projects. A Fortune 500 firm, AECOM companies, including URS Corporation, Tishman Construction and Hunt Construction Group, have annual revenue of approximately $18 billion.

Evolution of Transportation Management Centers (TMCs)

Over the years, transportation management centers (TMCs) have transformed from being single-dimensional (*e.g.,* focusing on signals, freeways, transit systems) to becoming more multi-jurisdictional and multi-modal. The "TMC of the Future" is anticipated to evolve in applying predictive models and automated decision support systems to stay ahead of congestion rather than reacting to it.

AECOM is a global leader in TMCs in all aspects of master planning, design, software development, systems integration, construction, and operations. Our forte is in the area of operations where we have worked in over 40 TMCs, thereby giving us an end-user's perspective of ITS and how to take it to the next level.

In Florida and California, we developed dynamic pricing software to operate their managed lanes networks. In Virginia, we designed, operated and maintained their reversible roadways systems. In New Jersey, we developed the next generation of Advanced Traffic Management System software to support predictive analytics and decision support systems. In Michigan, we are operating four TMCs where Connected Vehicle test beds are operating. In Missouri, we are operating the Gateway TMC in St. Louis which we anticipate will accommodate "Road to Tomorrow" innovations in the future.

Performance measures are reported on a monthly and annual basis for many of these TMCs. For example, the most recent annual report for the Florida DOT TMC in Miami shows a benefit-cost ratio of 53, meaning that for every dollar invested in the program, $53 is being returned in terms of travel time savings and safety benefits. This considers the fact that for every minute that a lane is blocked it translates to 4 minutes of delay and the probability of a secondary accident occurring increasing by 2.8 percent. Therefore, if you can clear the blocked lane 15 minutes faster, then you can avoid a one-hour delay and reduce the probability of a secondary accident occurring by over 40 percent.

Technology Partnerships and Smart Cities

The pace of change in this area creates a critical need for extensive technology partnerships. Innovation is occurring through these numerous and varied partnerships, and Federal, state, and local policy should do everything possible to encourage and facilitate continuation of dynamic partnering opportunities. Project sponsors need to pursue platforms that are flexible and will allow them to grow and develop over time as the community sets its priorities and develops its blueprint to guide future decision-making.

Strong and adaptive technology partnerships allow communities to build upon lessons-learned from previous efforts across the country. We recommend integrating the transportation technology strategy with the long-range regional transportation plan to connect the dots between existing conditions, forecast future conditions, and transformative technologies. Further, being creative and catalyzing new partnerships with the private sector is what enables adaptive solutions to be developed to new and changing challenges.

AECOM collaborates with many of the technology giants including Xerox with whom we developed the Los Angeles dynamic pricing system, and with IBM where we are developing software systems for the New Jersey Turnpike and collaborating on developing smart cities in India.

We were recently selected for the RoadX program in Colorado, and we are assisting the Missouri DOT on the "Road to Tomorrow" program in developing technology partnerships and innovations. In response to these emerging trends, the Colorado DOT is forming a technology-driven innovation venture called "RoadX". This initiative is aiming to make traveling in Colorado crash-free and delay-free, and will improve the efficiency of the state's transportation system within the next 10 years. The collaborative project focuses on building partnerships and entrepreneurial relationships that will deliver innovative solutions to reduce the cost of transporting goods, turn a rural state highway into a zero-death road, and improve congestion on Colorado's critical corridors. The program will employ a multi-pronged deployment, operations, innovation and technology approach with several efforts to be completed in the next five years. The Missouri DOT "Road to Tomorrow" program is looking at a broad suite of innovations including solar roadways, "Internet of Things" applications for smart traffic control, safety and road assistance, as well as smart pavement applications and truck platooning. Aggressive approaches to innovation such as these efforts require strong technology partnerships.

Internet of Things (IoT)

As no one owns the Internet, nor the controls and routes used to transmit data, the same could be said about the IoT. While there are 75 million servers running the global Internet, there are 1.2 billion cars driving global transportation (of which 20 percent are in the U.S.). Personal vehicle ownership is grossly inefficient: cars are estimated to be parked 95 percent of the time and our transportation systems are under-utilized during non-peak periods.

There is a reason the leading global Internet companies are looking at connected and automated vehicles as they understand the issues are similar to the decentralization of car ownership that created the Internet decades ago.

IoT approaches will allow people and cargo to be transported more efficiently across multimodal transportation networks at designated pickup and drop off times. This will enable the balancing of transportation supply and demand in real time by optimizing routes, modes, and schedules while eliminating human errors, thereby reducing accidents.

Working IoT strategies into our short and long-range transportation plans is a challenge. AECOM is currently supporting the New Zealand Transportation Authority in preparing them for connected and automated vehicles by assessing various scenarios of technology adoption rates and identifying the appropriate technology infrastructure improvements that will support it.

Innovations

In recent years, several innovations have surfaced to embed technology into our transportation systems to enable them to operate safer and more efficiently. Many DOTs have embraced a Transportation Systems Management & Operations approach which focuses on developing a higher level of operational integration across transportation modes while being aligned with performance measures used to improve operations. Other strategies include smart motorways, smart parking, data management, dynamic pricing, integrated corridor management, and electric vehicle charging systems. In addition to ITS, our "New Ventures" Practice seeks innovations in all aspects of our business such as the Hyperloop program which will eventually transport pods of people and cargo at speeds in excess of 700 mph. Meanwhile, smart cities, connected and automated vehicles have been receiving the most attention.

Examples of innovative projects where a great deal of the excitement is focused include:

- *Lake Tahoe Smart Parking:* This is a demonstration of how this technology improves the user's experience in mobility. Estimates indicate that 30 percent of urban congestion is created by people circling city streets looking for parking.

- *LA Metro Mobility Hubs:* The mobility hub model brings multiple technology-enabled transportation choices together in a single place to create a more streamlined experience for commuters, visitors or residents going about their daily business in the Los Angeles region. This project, funded by the Jobs Access Reverse Commute program, is also a way to make the benefits of a smarter transportation system accessible to those without access to the Internet at home.

- *Connected Vehicle Data Applications for TMCs:* Transportation agencies understand the importance of connected and automated vehicles and the impending emergence of this technology on the roads. AECOM is helping agencies figure out how to integrate this more holistically into the transportation ecosystem.

Each new innovation brings with it unique benefits, such as better management of infrastructure, and more responsive government services. Innovations can stretch limited resources to address greatest demand, bringing operational efficiencies that save taxpayers money, including:

- *On-demand services:* Improve garbage collection efficiency sending garbage trucks to collect trash based on sensors that indicate the need for service.

- *Waste reduction:* An estimated 2.1 trillion gallons of clean, treated water is lost every year to leaks in water infrastructure. For example, during 2013, Houston lost 15 percent of its water—15 billion gallons—to leaking pipes. Even aggressive efforts to fix leaks will not keep up with the rate of new leak formation. We need to better manage the flow of water by embedding sensors in water pipes throughout the distribution network which will save energy and water.

- *Optimized systems:* We can better manage storm water to minimize runoff and maximize capacity. Kansas City, Missouri is using sensors at critical points across the city for advance notification of potential flooding issues. Jacksonville, Florida is using a combination of cameras, sensors and analytics tools to quantify the passage of cars, pedestrians and bikes to measure the high rate of fatalities and injuries, inform planning staff of the need for new bike/pedestrian infrastructure as well as tracking and evaluating resulting behavior change, thereby increasing safety for pedestrians, cyclists and drivers.
- *Use of data to preempt and predict problems before they occur:* Infrastructure sensors can provide an ongoing assessment of the lifespan of major bridges, and even detect structural problems. For example, on the Brooklyn Bridge, sensors monitor cracks and temperature fluctuation.
- *Expanding the capacity of government to reach more people:* Digital kiosks in Kansas City and New York City, for example, are making it possible for citizens to access city services without needing to have access to smartphones or the Internet at home. This is essential in helping local government bridge the digital divide.
- *Better communication to stakeholders:* This includes real-time tracking of transportation (where is my bus) and other services such as snow plows (when will my street be plowed). When Pennsylvania was hit with a major snow storm last year that crippled traffic on the interstates, the DOT used its partnership with Google Waze to provide information to drivers stuck in traffic/snow when the highways were shut down

TMC of the Future

I would like to leave you with my vision for the "TMC of the Future". While the "TMC of the Present" continues to focus on our core functions related to traffic operations and safety (*i.e.,* incident, traffic, special event, and work zone management); and the "TMC of the Future" will accommodate next generation ITS strategies (*e.g.,* active traffic management, managed lanes, integrated corridor management, connected vehicles, predictive modelling, decision support systems); the Internet of Things has the potential for integrating transportation operations with other city services (*e.g.,* smart parking, public safety, smart buildings, security, air quality, emergency management, water & waste water management, and smart energy grid systems).

While this integration may be virtual or a physical collocation of operations staff, and there are pros and cons to each approach, the integration has the potential to open new ways to apply the IoT and big data to utilize our transportation resources to its highest and best use while enabling the user to customize their trips based on their specific needs and desires. I suggest that consideration be made to incorporating the "TMC of the Future" concept into Smart Cities.

Enabling Policies

Innovation is occurring at an incredibly rapid pace across this country. To address these changes, and continue to foster innovation, Congress may wish to consider the following:

Revisiting policies at the Federal and state levels to attract technology partnerships. For example, public-private partnerships may be considered where the auto manufacturers/original equipment manufacturers (OEMs) build new capacity (*e.g.,* an additional traffic lane) to accommodate autonomous vehicles. As the penetration of autonomous vehicles grows over time, more vehicles would likely use this dedicated lane. Funding for all infrastructure remains a challenge. Through the current available and developing technologies, it would be possible to enable the assessment of user fees which would generate revenue to offset the costs of construction, operations and maintenance. This also opens the possibility for revenue sharing arrangements that could expedite the phase in of autonomous vehicles while generating revenue for both parties.

Relieving regulatory constraints that may hinder implementation of new technologies. Much of our public policy is built around the technologies of the past and can make it difficult to introduce new alternatives. This is particularly relevant when you think about how cities function—if an inspector has access to real-time data in the field, he or she may be empowered to make different decisions than if he were to simply respond to the issue at hand.

Providing expanded funding for "Smart City" grants to allow more cities to participate across the Nation. As 78 cities applied for the USDOT Smart City Challenge grant, and only one (Columbus) was selected, the interest in these technology developments is significant, and demand for resources is high. Dedicated resources for Smart Cities would provide an expanded national showcase of how IoT and big data can be applied in a diverse range of applications. Federal funding for the implementation of new technology applications can remove the risk for project sponsors and provides technology partners (large and small) the opportunity for a return on investment to cover their R&D costs.

Provide Federal funding for programs similar to RoadX (Colorado) and Road to Tomorrow (Missouri). These programs are seeking technology partnerships to innovate new technologies and apply them to our transportation systems. While RoadX is funded by the Colorado DOT, the Road to Tomorrow is primarily reliant on revenue generated from new sources and innovative partnering strategies. New grant programs (such as the nationally significant freight and highway (FASTLANE) grant program included in the FAST Act can be helpful, as can funding provided through the TIGER Grant Program. At the end of the day, sustainable revenue streams are critical for major innovations to be implemented in meaningful ways.

Areas for Future Focus/Opportunities

Standardization is critical: This will further help the scalability of these solutions: data management (ownership, sharing, privacy, security and future monetization strategies).

Open architecture and interoperability of systems: It is important to maintain flexibility to adapt systems over time as technology evolves so quickly. Communities need to be sure that they are building a platform that can adapt as the technology changes.

Workforce Development: Managing digital infrastructure requires new skill sets and there is a foundational need to focus on digital literacy at all levels within government (from the field technician to supervisors and management). We need to build local capacity for data analysis which requires the ability to contract with and hire talent equipped for the new world of big data.

Closing

On behalf of AECOM, I would like to thank you for receiving my testimony and look forward to addressing your questions.

How the Internet of Things can bring U.S. Transportation and Infrastructure into the 21st Century

United States Senate
COMMITTEE ON COMMERCE, SCIENCE, AND TRANSPORTATION

Dr. Robert Edelstein, PE
Senior Vice President

AECOM
Built to deliver a better world

AECOM

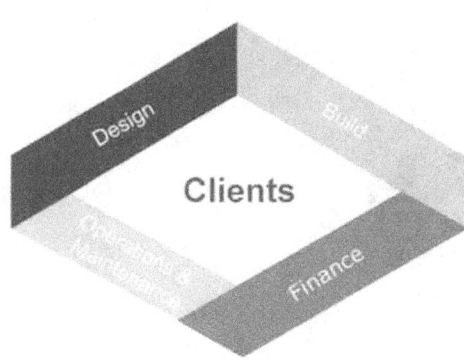

- Fortune 500 Firm
- ENR Ranking #1
- 150 Countries
- 92,000 Employees
- $18 Billion Revenue

AECOM
Built to deliver a better world

Transportation Management Centers

Florida   Virginia   Michigan

California   New Jersey   Missouri

AECOM
Built to deliver a better world

Technology Partnerships

AECOM
Built to deliver a better world

Internet of Things

Internet Protocol	75M Servers 1.2B Cars	Unused Capacity
Share Transport Resources		Connected & Automated Vehciles
Designated Pickup/Dropoff	Packets of People & Cargo	Decentralize Car Ownership

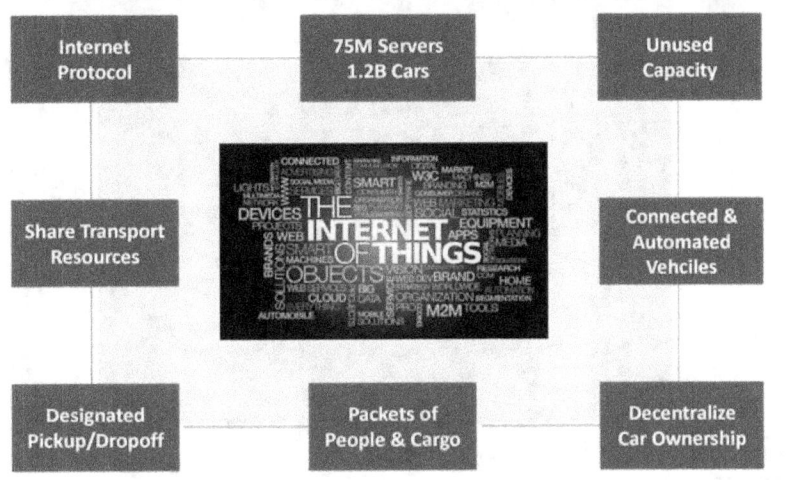

AECOM
Built to deliver a better world

Innovations

TSM&O

Smart Truck Parking

Integrated Corridor Management

Smart Cities

Smart Motorways

Data Management Systems

Hyperloop

Connected Vehicles

Smart Parking Systems

Dynamic Pricing

Electric Vehicle Charging

Automated Vehicles

AECOM
Built to deliver a better world

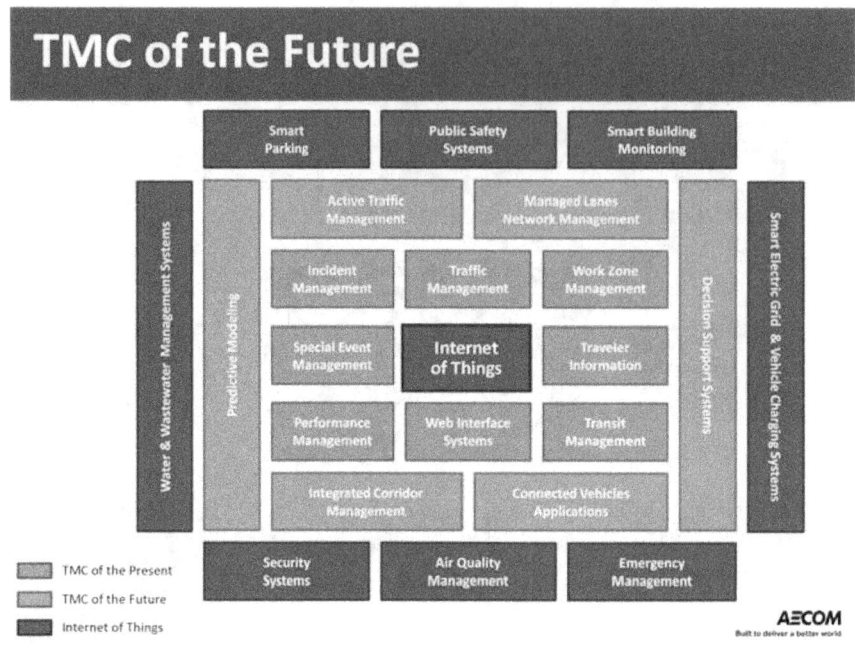

TMC of the Present
TMC of the Future
Internet of Things

AECOM
Built to deliver a better world

Senator FISCHER. Thank you very much.

Next, Mr. Jordan Kass, the President of Managed Services at C.H. Robinson. Welcome.

STATEMENT OF JORDAN KASS, PRESIDENT OF MANAGED SERVICES, C.H. ROBINSON

Mr. KASS. Chairman Fischer, Ranking Member Booker, and members of the Commerce, Science, and Transportation Committee, thank you for the opportunity to testify at today's hearing.

As one of the Nation's largest third-party logistics providers, C.H. Robinson has a unique view of how goods and commerce flow from manufacturer to consumer. My name is Jordan Kass, and I am President of Managed Services for C.H. Robinson. I joined Robinson in 1999 by way of an acquisition.

At that time, I created a startup within Robinson trying to figure out how to leverage Internet technology within the supply chain. Today, that startup business manages over $3 billion of logistics spend in 170 different countries on behalf of our customers. Our mission is to develop innovative technology platforms paired with managed services that help our customers connect, automate, and optimize their supply chains.

C.H. Robinson has over 150 offices around the world networked through our common proprietary platform called Navisphere, which provides our employees, our customers, and our carriers visibility to freight shipments around the country and globe.

Today, we are also speaking on behalf of the Transportation Intermediaries Association, which represents 1,500 3PLs of all sizes.

We do not own any commercial trucks ourselves, but build technology platforms and logistics services that streamline complex transportation management on behalf of our customers. Our diverse carrier base includes motor carriers, railroads, airfreight, and ocean carriers.

The division of Robinson that I lead works with some of the largest companies in the world, and this platform that we have developed serves as the platform these companies use to gain visibility and control over our supply chain. Our customers include companies like Microsoft, Delphi Automotive, and Ocean Spray.

A major component of our value proposition is routing massive amounts of information and money quickly and accurately around the world. This is enabled by technology and automation. From the truck driver using our cell phone app to find available loads to the customer who needs to find desired landed costs tracked to the item level, data and the Internet of Things is driving change in our business. We are rapidly expanding these tools and information available to all trading partners across the supply chain.

For example, a single truck owner-operator uses our app to check in like a GPS-equipped truck, and similarly a global shipper can view tracking updates anywhere in the world via a PC, smart phone, or tablet.

Businesses today are part of global cross-functional teams of coordinating production, customer service, sales, finance, and transportation. They work together toward an end goal of customer experience and agile market response.

As Congress considers the implications an increasingly connected world has on policy, we see things differently, from a supply chain and flow of goods viewpoint.

Today, others have discussed privacy and IT infrastructure. However, we think that Congress also needs to look at practical issues regarding freight movement brought about by the Internet of Things. We fully understand that the Subcommittee does not have jurisdiction over all the issues I will mention. However, the Internet of Things forces us to look holistically with our customers at end-to-end supply chain practices. We want to reiterate that the greatest challenge Congress and subcommittees may have with the Internet of Things is that it will force the government to work across silos or be left behind by more agile governments. The following are our recommendations.

First, tax rates. Many of the companies leading the revolution around the Internet of Things are operating with a tax code designed for the 1980s. For example, C.H. Robinson is a service company with no assets and we pay full U.S. corporate tax of 35 percent. Even though we are 208 on the Fortune 500, we are a Fortune 100 corporate taxpayer. If Congress wishes to incubate globally leading countries, a corporate tax reform is a prerequisite.

World-class customer customs agency. We see the U.S. customs clearance process as a significant risk to supply chains. When the ACE system goes down for 2 hours during produce season in San Diego, it impacts supply chains across the Nation. Congress needs to make sure our U.S. customs agency provides world-class service and works well with agencies to ensure safe and efficient movement of goods.

Increasing resources for cargo theft deterrence. Cargo thieves are using the Internet to target specific freight. Law enforcement is challenged to investigate cargo thefts and victims in many locations. A stolen load of almonds may originate in California, be stolen in Nevada on a truck based out of Missouri. We recommend increasing penalties for cargo theft and providing law enforcement resources to fund cargo-theft specific units.

Land use and planning around the rise of megacities. Increasingly, freight moves between a handful of global cities seeing huge population and density growth, including Chicago, Houston, New York, and LA. Issues of land use, truck parking, congestion, vehicle size, and operating hours all interact with the growth of things and the speed of change of delivery direct to the consumer.

Thank you for the opportunity to provide insight into how the Internet of Things is impacting supply chains. We look forward to working with the Committee on policy that allows U.S. logistics companies to continue leading the world.

[The prepared statement of Mr. Kass follows:]

PREPARED STATEMENT OF JORDAN KASS, PRESIDENT OF MANAGED SERVICES, C. H. ROBINSON ON BEHALF OF TRANSPORTATION INTERMEDIARIES ASSOCIATION

Chairwoman Fischer, Ranking Member Booker, and members of the Commerce, Science and Transportation Committee, thank you for the invitation and the opportunity to testify at today's hearing. As one of the Nation's largest third party logistics providers, C. H. Robinson has a unique view of how goods and commerce flow from manufacturer to consumer. The transportation brokerage and third party logistics industries have grown substantially the last 10 years and I will provide you an overview of our role in the marketplace and policy recommendations to consider around the Internet of Things as it relates specifically to supply chains.

Introduction of Jordan Kass

My name is Jordan Kass and I am the President of Managed Services for C. H. Robinson. I joined C.H. Robinson in 1999 via the way of an acquisition. At that time I created a startup within the framework of CH Robinson. You may recall that was the peak of the dot.com boom and everyone was trying to figure out how to leverage Internet technology. The business I began for CH Robinson was focused on bringing the Internet into the world of logistics and supply chain. Today, that business has grown tremendously and we manage over $3Billion dollars of logistics spend in 170 different countries on behalf of our customers. Our mission is to develop innovative technology platforms paired with managed services that help our customers connect, automate, and optimize their supply chains.

Introduction of C.H. Robinson

C. H. Robinson was founded in 1905 and facilitates the movement of over 17 million shipments per year. We have been named the #1 3PL for five years in a row by Inbound Logistics magazine and have pioneered many industry innovations. We are also speaking today on behalf of the Transportation Intermediaries Association, which represents 1500 3PL's of all sizes. C.H. Robinson is a leading member of TIA and serve on their board of directors. C.H. Robinson is the 10th largest publicly held company headquartered in Minnesota, and we have over 150 offices across the United States. All of our offices are networked through a common proprietary platform, called Navisphere, which provides our employees, our customers and our contracted carriers' visibility to freight shipments across the country and across the globe regardless of mode.

We are a Fortune 250 company with annual revenues of more than $13.5 billion serving manufacturing, retail and wholesale customers of all types across the economic spectrum. We do not own any commercial trucks ourselves, but rather build technology platforms and logistics services that allow us to streamline complex transportation management on behalf of our customers. We have developed the largest and most diverse carrier base in the U.S. in order to transport our customer's freight. Our carrier base includes motor carriers, railroads, air freight, and ocean carriers. Leveraging our technology platform, our expert talent worked with approximately 68,000 transportation providers in 2015.

As I mentioned, the division of C.H. Robinson that I lead is focused on delivering technology and services that connect, automate, and optimize global supply chains. We work with some of the largest companies in the world and our platform serves as the technology these companies use to gain visibility and control over their supply chain. Our customers include companies like Microsoft, Delphi, John Deere, and Ocean Spray.

A major component of our value proposition is to route massive amounts of information and money quickly and accurately around the world. Our platform vis-à-vis the Internet formulates the information and visibility pipes our customers require. Again, I want to emphasize that we do this on a massive scale.

This is enabled by increasingly sophisticated technology and automation across the supply chain. From the truck driver using a cell phone to search for available loads on our Navisphere Carrier app to railroads sending massive tracking data in electronic formats to customers desiring to know landed costs tracked to the item level, data and the Internet of Things is driving incremental change in our business. One example of the massive role data plays can be seen in our every increasing machine to machine communication. Every day, C.H. Robinson transmits and receives over 20 million electronic communications.

We are rapidly expanding the tools and information available to all trading partners across the supply chain. For example, single truck owner operators can use our app to perform a tracking check call just like a GPS equipped truck without ever picking up the phone and similarly a global shipper can view that tracking update anywhere in the world via a phone, PC, or tablet.

Businesses and transportation departments are part of global cross functional teams coordinating sophisticated supply chains across many silos. Production, customer service, sales, finance and transportation all work together towards an end goal of customer experience and agile market response. As Congress rightly considers the implications of how an increasingly connected world impacts policy and society, we would like to provide insights we see from a supply chain and flow of goods viewpoint. While other witnesses will discuss issues of privacy, security, and IT infrastructure, there are many practical issues Congress should also consider regarding supply chain changes coming from the Internet of Things and how U.S. companies can lead in this industry.

We fully understand that this subcommittee does not have jurisdiction over all the issues we will mention. However, the Internet of Things crosses many of our company's silos and has forced us to look holistically with our customers at end-to-end supply chain practices. We want to reiterate that the greatest challenge Congress and this subcommittee may have with the development of the Internet of Things is that it will force the U.S. Government to break down silos and work in cross-functional teams or be left behind for smaller countries and more agile governments to lead the way. Following are recommendations the Internet of Things working should consider:

Tax Rates

Many of the company's leading the revolution around the Internet of Things are operating with a tax code designed for manufacturing in the 1980s. For example, C.H. Robinson is primarily a service company with no assets and we pay the full U.S. corporate tax rate of 35 percent annually in addition to state taxes. Even though we are #208 on the Fortune 500, we are a Fortune 100 corporate taxpayer when the Fortune 500 is ranked in terms of raw corporate tax paid. Over the last 11 years, our company alone has paid more than $2 billion in Federal corporate tax.

- If Congress wishes to promote and incubate globally leading companies in the Internet of things based in the US, corporate tax reform is a pre-requisite.

World Class U.S Customs Agency

The Internet of Things provides companies the ability to source parts and inputs and sell globally. Consumers can now buy directly from overseas retailers and manufacturers and with the increase in the de minimis value by Congress from $200 to $800, we increasingly see the U.S. Customs clearance process as a significant risk to supply chains. When the ACE system goes down for 2 hours during produce season in San Diego, or U.S. EPA holds up a shipment at the port of Baltimore because they are understaffed, it impacts supply chains across the Nation. Just as successful companies are now forced to work across silos, one of the biggest challenges that the Internet of Things will place on the U.S. Government is on the customs service and their coordination with other government agencies of all types.

- Congress needs to make sure our U.S. Customs agency provides world class services and that they are able to work well across agencies to ensure a safe and efficient movement of goods or the U.S. will not hold a leadership position regarding the Internet of Things.

Increasing Resources for Cargo Theft Deterrence

While many will be focused on personal privacy and the data collected on individuals through the Internet of Things, please also remember to strengthen cargo theft penalties. One of the unintended consequences of increased technology in the supply chain is the increased ability of cargo thieves to target specific freight across the country. Law enforcement is challenged to prioritize and investigate cargo thefts with victims and stakeholders in many diverse locations. For example, a stolen load of almonds may originate in California, be stolen in Nevada, on a truck based out of Missouri and brokered by a company in Chicago.

- We recommend that Congress increase penalties for cargo theft and provide law enforcement resources to fund local and regional cargo theft specific law enforcement units.

Land Use and Planning around the rise of Mega Cities

A trend that we are monitoring closely is the trend of megacities. Increasingly, freight movement is concentrated in and between a handful of global cities that are seeing huge population and density growth, including cities in the U.S. like Chicago, Houston, New York, and Los Angeles. Providing goods to these urban populations is a growing logistics challenge Congress should monitor and prioritize. Issues of land use, truck parking, congestion, vehicle size, and operating hours all interact with the growth of the Internet of Things and the speed of change of delivery directly to the consumer.

Thank you for the opportunity to provide insight into how big data and the Internet of Things is impacting supply chains. We commend the Committee on their focus on this important topic, but emphasize that the rate of change in the market continues to accelerate. We look forward to working with the Committee and the working groups established by this legislation to quickly and specifically identify policy areas that will allow U.S. companies to continue to lead the world.

Senator FISCHER. Thank you very much to the entire panel. We will begin our first round of questions, 5 minutes for each member.

I would like to start with one issue that I've been concerned about, and that is the creation of these regulatory silos. I'm worried about the lack of coordination between government agencies where we may see duplication take place, and cross purposes happen on this with regulations.

When my Ranking Member and I and two other Senators introduced the DIGIT Act, one thing we wanted to be sure to do was have a working group created, and we did that. That is a working group with government and also private stakeholders. And we want to make sure that we can look at streamlining and having complementary regulations between agencies when we address the Internet of Things.

So I would like to ask all the members of the panel, what do you believe is causing these regulatory silos? And what do you think is the best way that we can encourage cooperation among agencies in order to look at how best to allow that innovation and creativity to continue to take place with the Internet of Things?

Who would like to start? Yes, Doctor?

Dr. EDELSTEIN. I think the departments of transportation, including the U.S. Department of Transportation, have already taken that first step. That first step is really transportation systems management and operations, or TSM&O. The way I look at it, with

TSM&O and IoT, when those two worlds collide, it is going to unleash really unlimited potential.

Transportation systems management and operations is creating operational integration between the various modal partners, whether it be buses, trains, toll roads, freeways, or arterial operations. It is also aligned with performance metrics so everybody has some skin in the game with regard to defining those performance metrics, tracking those performance metrics, and making sure we are making certain improvements that are noticeable by the end-user, which is that the traveler.

So, again, it's not a regulatory issue, but it is more of an operational issue, and I think that it is starting to come together rather quickly in many States throughout the country.

Senator FISCHER. Mr. Davis?

Mr. DAVIS. Chairwoman Fischer, I think you are asking a great question. Let me touch on a couple things.

First, I want to applaud the work that has been done on the DIGIT Act and the goals that that is trying to achieve. I think that is a very important direction for us to be taking with regard to the Internet of Things.

You asked an interesting question about the history in terms of why we have these silos, and I think it's really been because of the optimization that has been needed in those various different industries. We want to optimize what is happening in shipping, optimize what is happening in retail, in the network infrastructure, so I think that's been a very natural kind of evolution.

But as we think forward around the Internet of Things, that will be one of our challenges to scale, to have these local optimizations, because we are seeing that these technologies needed to create the connectivity between things and the data center or cloud will need to become more and more common.

That is why we are advocating the implementation of open platforms to allow for much greater flexibility to break down some of those silos. That will be essential for the Internet of Things to be able to scale.

We look at 5G technologies. We look at what we are trying to accomplish across the industries with regard to security. These things are going to have to become much more open. They're going to have to be driven by public-private partnerships to define the right capabilities. That is what is going to enable scalability as we go forward in the Internet of Things.

Senator FISCHER. Do you think we are going to have to see a collision take place before we will have that openness? Or will we be proactive in trying to head it off before we get there?

Mr. DAVIS. Well, obviously, I am hoping that we can be proactive and avoid a collision, but I think that is really why it is important to think about this globally and think about what is happening in other parts of the world and have that national IoT strategy for the U.S. to really be in a leadership position to help shape how that evolves.

I think as far as we can think ahead and be proactive, that will avoid that ultimate collision.

Senator FISCHER. Thank you. I'm running out of time, but if the other three witnesses can give me a short answer?

Yes?

Mr. MONJE. Senator, your question is exactly right. It's something that we've been driven to do by the White House directives.

We are working very closely with the Federal Trade Commission when it comes to privacy. They are in charge, but we have a huge stake in it, and we're working very closely with them, the national NTIA on issues of cybersecurity broadband access, and the FCC when it comes to spectrum.

We are not only reaching across the Federal Government but also down into the States as well. NHTSA is establishing their regulatory framework working very closely with the States, because what you don't want to have is patchwork.

Senator FISCHER. OK.

Ms. Reynolds, did you have a comment?

Ms. REYNOLDS. I appreciate the question. Obviously, government silos are nothing new. They are something that we have struggled with for quite a long time. I think that what it really comes down to is the way that we measure success is often at odds.

To Dr. Edelstein's point about having a shared performance metric and hearing a clear signal, which we've heard from U.S. DOT and the Federal Government, that the road to funding is paved with partnerships and that if you want to be at the table, you need to bring private partners along with you, you need to bring the State, you need to bring your region, are really bringing up some very uncomfortable sacred cows that we have to wrestle with.

So I think that is one of the major ways that there has been kind of a happily forced arranged marriage among different sectors of the public and private side.

Senator FISCHER. And, Mr. Kass, shortly, if you could condense?

Mr. KASS. My expertise is supply chain and technology. It's not government. So having said that——

Senator FISCHER. You're the best one to answer the question.

[Laughter.]

Mr. KASS. Having said that, as I said in my testimony, these walls need to be broken down. If we don't do this, what's going to happen—there are two supply chains at work. There is a physical one and a virtual one. The virtual supply chain is about moving information and money. In the Internet of Things, that's going to be visible. If we don't fix this problem, all of the problems that exist today, the nodes, the failure nodes, those are going to be exposed on a massive scale. So we have to get out in front of this and get out in front of it quickly.

Senator FISCHER. Thank you very much.

Senator Booker?

Senator BOOKER. Thank you very much.

When I was Mayor of my city, I discovered, in just getting accountability for my team members, that if I started encouraging constituents to tweet at me problems, that I would begin to find out about things. And it worked better than I knew. I could find out about potholes before my road engineers. I could find out about traffic lights out. I started crowdsourcing what was going wrong in the city. Obviously, that's a very rudimentary, inefficient way, when you can set up cities like Los Angeles where you could have sensors detecting problems and funneling information at the speed of light. So the Smart Cities Initiative to me, as a former Mayor, is really exciting.

Would you please give Mayor Garcetti my best when you get back to Los Angeles? I studied with him at Oxford. He still owes me 10 pounds. At this point, it's worth only like $.50, the way the pound is going.

[Laughter.]

Senator BOOKER. But tell him I want my money.

Would you tell me what kind of challenges you guys are facing in implementing what is a cutting-edge vision to try to make Los Angeles—what are the biggest obstacles to being a smart city that you are finding?

Ms. REYNOLDS. So thank you for the question. I will say it is two things.

One, fundamentally, public and private sides are going to have to get way outside our comfort zones in order to achieve the kind of partnership that we need. Our procurement practices, for example, I would say, are probably the single biggest hurdle to really getting public partners to the table. As soon as it takes us 18 or 24 months to write a request for proposals and bring a vendor on board, the technology has passed us by. The Federal Transit Administration and others have done a really good job signaling that they are willing to waive some of the Federal procurement requirements to allow cities to have access to these funds. I would identify that.

Second, I would say that the role of government—our most rudimentary tool is that we can say no. I think that oftentimes we find ourselves in that position when we are encountering the sort of disruption or introduction of new technologies in transportation in our cities. We need to pivot to using one of the other sort of lesser used powers of government, which is to bring people together, to convene, possibly to regulate, and to make sure that the price of entry into our cities is that you have to serve them equitably.

I will just give one example. Mayor Garcetti executed a data-sharing agreement with Waze. One in four drivers in the City of Los Angeles is using Waze to get around our city with positive and potentially negative impacts.

The way we have been using it is bringing Waze data into our ATSAC system, fusing the data streams that we have to make our system even smarter. We save Los Angeles drivers over 40 hours every year because we have a smart transportation signal system.

That is just the tip of the iceberg, and it points to the other big challenge, which is that we don't have the skillsets inside government. I don't have a civil service classification for data scientists in the City of Los Angeles, and we desperately need those kinds of skillsets and capacity-building inside government so that we can really come to the table as an equal partner.

Senator BOOKER. I appreciate that. That is what the White House is finding out with their innovation team. Procurement is one of the biggest problems we have. The procurement process is set up for dealing with big, massive companies, not the small innovators who are at the cutting edge. I appreciate that.

In the 1 minute and 30 seconds I have left, Mr. Kass, Mr. Davis, I get very annoyed when I watch other countries who are beginning to out-innovate us. We should be the innovation capital of the globe. I'm a competitive guy. I want us to be number one.

But when I see government regulations choking things like the drone industry, for example, in watching innovation in that sector go over to Europe as opposed to here because we haven't created an environment that is best for that. So to the two men who are in the private sector, could you guys just tell me what are other countries doing better than us that we should be doing better than them?

Mr. DAVIS. I think it's a great point. That is one of the reasons we have been advocating for public-private partnerships, to be able to bring private industry alongside what is happening from a regulatory standpoint as well as what is happening in areas like academia, to be able to provide those kinds of partnerships to go off and define what needs to happen. Again, the emphasis is on what as opposed to the very specific how of the implementation.

That is what we often find ends up happening when we try to put regulation in place too early as the technology is still rapidly evolving. We should agree on what we are trying to accomplish as opposed to the very specific implementation.

That is one of the things that we find as we look at what is happening globally, the opportunity to innovate much more openly.

Senator BOOKER. Jordan, why don't you hold on, because I want to be respectful to Senator Cantwell. She is a dear friend, and I don't want to make her angry, and I'll let her go. We will come around to another round.

Mr. KASS. Yes. No problem.

Senator FISCHER. Senator Cantwell?

STATEMENT OF HON. MARIA CANTWELL, U.S. SENATOR FROM WASHINGTON

Senator CANTWELL. Thank you, Madam Chair. And thank you to the panelists.

Is it Monje?

Mr. MONJE. Monje.

Senator CANTWELL. Monje. Thank you so much for your work.

I wanted to talk to you and Mr. Davis about freight because this is something we want to be strategic about in the United States. The opportunity to ship more goods to markets overseas from the U.S. is a very important economic strategy for us, but it has to move in a timely fashion. And obviously, there are lots of challenges.

So how is the Department of Transportation—we have had this strategic freight plan—working with the Internet of Things? We had I think it was one of the California ports here last year, and they talked about the efficiencies that you can roll out at our ports by having this kind of data and information on cargo movements and on trucks.

Mr. MONJE. Yes, ma'am. Thank you for the question.

Freight is the lifeblood of our economy, and this Congress has been on the record in really pushing us as a department to come up with a strategic plan to work with States.

In terms of the Internet of Things, it has tremendous potential. We know we are going to see 45 percent more freight over the next

30 years on our roads, on our ports, across our seaways. Some of the things we are doing include testing and improving the quality of the technology called FRATIS, which we are implementing at the Ports of Long Beach and Los Angeles, and it is helping operators get cargo off ships and to where they need to go a lot quicker.

We have a connected vehicle pilot in Wyoming that is really focused on speeding truck traffic along Interstate 80, which has major weather events. So how are we using technology to move that forward?

As part of our Smart City Challenge, we actually got a lot of really neat examples of communities that are trying to figure this out for themselves. Columbus is proposing, and they won, so they are going to be able to implement, the ability to practice truck platooning along smart corridors, better ways to do urban parking.

One of the neater ideas that came is from Austin, which is actually looking at shared urban delivery lockers, so people as they get off the bus will be able to pick up their groceries or a package, and they don't have to make an extra trip to get there.

So we are doing a lot of foundational research in the maritime area. We know that this is a tremendous area of opportunity, and that we need to be partners in that process.

Senator CANTWELL. Mr. Davis, I think the average tractor-trailer gets something like 6 miles per gallon, so anything we can do to increase the fuel efficiency there is going to be a huge savings.

I know that, again, DOT has SuperTruck. Is that what you were referring to? The SuperTruck program? I didn't get the acronym you used.

Mr. DAVIS. FRATIS is what I referred to.

Senator CANTWELL. How do you spell that?

Mr. DAVIS. F-R-A-T-I-S.

Senator CANTWELL. OK. Well, I also know that you have a SuperTruck program, and it is focused on getting more like nine, almost 10 miles per gallon. So how do you think that some of these tools could be used to help the transportation sector on timing on deliveries?

Mr. DAVIS. I think we've seen some really exciting technologies in the early stages. I think that Mr. Monje talked about a couple. Mr. Kass even described a few, which is to be able to put technologies in trucks that enable us to understand how they are being driven and to be able to provide feedback to the driver about he or she can drive more efficiently.

We have seen this implemented in a couple of large trucking firms already, and they see some of those pretty impressive improvements in fuel efficiency. I think that is one.

We are seeing technologies evolve that allow us to be very cost-effectively identify the location and the conditions of high-value freight so that we know where it is, we know what kind of conditions it is being subjected to.

And then to be able to use autonomous technologies, to be able to identify maybe containers that are coming in on a ship with where trucks are located to be able to synchronize the way they are offloaded to take advantage of the trucks or the traffic conditions to move that material effectively.

So we are seeing some very interesting early stage technologies. The challenge is how we make that more and more common across all of those applications to enable it to scale.

Senator CANTWELL. I think we learned in air transportation now that there is a cell lot and everybody hangs out in the cell lot.

I think that statistic is quite impressive, a 45 percent increase in freight traffic. I mean, we want the United States to make things. We want to sell things. We want to move them. But the congestion level at the ports is so great, so a strategy that could ease that traffic in there and move it in a more systematic way would mean huge savings and would help us with our competitiveness in manufacturing, so I hope that we will stick with it.

Thank you, Madam Chair.

Senator FISCHER. Thank you.

Senator Markey?

STATEMENT OF HON. EDWARD MARKEY,
U.S. SENATOR FROM MASSACHUSETTS

Senator MARKEY. Thank you, Madam Chair.

The Internet of Things leads also to the Internet of threats, because, obviously, every device that has the Internet built into it then becomes subject to hacking. That's just the bottom line. So you have to basically deal with the digital tale of two technologies. It is the best of technologies, it is the worst of technologies simultaneously.

So if you don't deal with threats, then all you are doing is ignoring the inevitable problems that are going to be created.

So really, today's new cars are just computers on wheels. That's all they really have become. That is why in 2013, and again last year, Senator Blumenthal and I asked 20 automakers what they are doing to protect our computers on wheels, and here is what we learned.

Thieves no longer need a crowbar to break into your car. They just need an iPhone.

Last year, we witnessed firsthand how easily cars could be hacked. We watched as hackers remotely took control of the brakes, the steering, and the acceleration of a Jeep Cherokee. Chrysler had to recall 1.4 million vehicles to fix this cybersecurity problem.

But in this new Internet of Things era, cybersecurity just cannot be an afterthought. Rather than addressing cybersecurity problems after a hack has occurred, we have to ensure robust cybersecurity protections are built into these technologies right from the beginning.

That means that we need enforceable rules of the road to protect driver privacy and security. That is why I introduced legislation with Senator Blumenthal, the Security and Privacy in Your Car act, or SPY Car Act, that directs the National Highway Traffic Safety Administration and the Federal Trade Commission to establish Federal standards to secure our cars and protect our drivers.

So for all the panelists, please, answer yes or no. Do you believe that cars should have mandatory cybersecurity standards, including hacking protections to protect all access points in a car; data security measures that prevent unwanted access to all collected information; and hacking mitigation technologies that can detect, report, and stop hacking attempts in real-time?

Dr. Edelstein?

Dr. EDELSTEIN. Definitely, yes.

Senator MARKEY. Yes. OK.

Mr. Davis?

Mr. DAVIS. Definitely yes. The one thing I would add is that I think it is important to define what we need to accomplish to address the things that you described, but also to allow technology to evolve quickly.

Senator MARKEY. But if it evolves and it is still not installed, we should mandate that is installed?

Mr. DAVIS. Yes, we should define requirements to ensure these things are secure.

Senator MARKEY. Mr. Kass?

Mr. KASS. Yes, we need the appropriate controls, but I agree we need to do it in a very balanced way that doesn't kill innovation.

Innovation is like a whack-a-mole, right? You try to beat it down, it is just going to pop up someplace else. So we really need a way, a mechanism, of ensuring that if we are going to put controls in place, that it is not offsetting the innovation that is about to take place, but rather helping it and making sure it thrives.

Senator MARKEY. But haven't you found over the years, Mr. Kass, that if people can get away without building in the protections against hacking or privacy, that they just do it to save money?

Mr. KASS. People never cease to amaze me.

Senator MARKEY. Thank you so much. So it's not just whack-a-mole. It's just whack-a-bad-person.

Mr. KASS. Well, no, I was speaking of innovation. We can't policy our way out of it. Someone is going to innovate, and it needs to be us. We need to lead.

Senator MARKEY. Right. We have to do it, but at the same time, we then have to tell people who don't want to install the safety protections that they have to do it.

Mr. KASS. Fair enough.

Senator MARKEY. OK, thank you. That's all I'm really saying. And, Ms. Reynolds?

Ms. REYNOLDS. I think the answer is certainly yes, and I will add that there is a role for smart infrastructure as well. One of the few benefits to having started our connected signal system in the 1980s is that it is all hard fiber and it is virtually unhackable. There will be a role for infrastructure to manage not just the hacking but the 12 or 20 different vehicle software technologies that are out there.

Senator MARKEY. But again, I didn't get the correct answer from the auto manufacturers.

Ms. REYNOLDS. Yes.

Senator MARKEY. Thank you so much. I mean, seatbelts are good but not just yet. Airbag is good, but not just yet. We just want the technology to evolve a little bit more. So when, Lord, will you put those seatbelts, those airbags, those hacking protections in?

Mr. Monje?

Mr. MONJE. Thank you, Senator. And thank you for your leadership on this issue.

You know, cybersecurity is going to be a continuous challenge for the rest of this century. There is substantial motivation on our part to get it right on behalf of safety, certainly from the manufacturers.

NHTSA is doing everything we can. We have established standards, a security credential management system for V2V technology to ensure that those packets of information can be shared safely. We are going to continue to work with industry, continue to work with experts to make sure we continue to fight this threat.

Senator MARKEY. Dr. Edelstein—if I can just have one more minute, please? Thank you.

Do you believe also that we should make owners explicitly aware of collection, transmission, retention, and use of driving data and provide owners the right to say no to data collection and retention without losing access to key navigation or other features?

Dr. EDELSTEIN. Yes.

Senator MARKEY. Yes.

Mr. Davis?

Mr. DAVIS. Yes.

Senator MARKEY. Yes.

Mr. Kass?

Mr. KASS. Yes. And just generally speaking, with all the information that is going to be available, this concept of opting out I think is important.

Senator MARKEY. Excellent, thank you.

Ms. Reynolds?

Ms. REYNOLDS. Yes.

Senator MARKEY. Excellent.

Mr. MONJE. Yes, sir. It's very important to only collect the information you need and make sure consumers know what they are sharing.

Senator MARKEY. Thank you.

So I think that is a great balance here. It's not all good. Like any other technology, there is the bad as well. And we just have to make sure that we build in the protections at the same time that we build in the opportunities. And if we do that, then I think we discharge our responsibility as policymakers.

I thank you, Madam Chair, Mr. Ranking Member, for this hearing.

Senator FISCHER. Thank you, Senator Markey.

Dr. Edelstein, in your written testimony, you discuss several innovative transportation projects that you are currently working on.

For example, you mentioned that AECOM employs sensors to monitor the Brooklyn Bridge for cracks and also for temperature fluctuation. What is the impact of real-time data monitoring on our Nation's critical transportation infrastructure assets, especially as it relates to public spending on maintenance?

Dr. EDELSTEIN. We're not monitoring the Brooklyn Bridge. That was a case example that other people are doing, but it has nothing to do with AECOM. I just wanted to get that out.

Again, my vision for the control centers of the future, I really see it getting into not only moving people and cargo more efficiently, but also asset management in real-time. This way we can put sensors out on our bridges. We can monitor smart buildings with regard to energy systems. We can put sensors out on water systems to see if there are any potential leaks in the pipes that will cause inefficiency.

So what I am looking at is a control center—again, it can be a virtual control center; it doesn't have to be one massive building— a control center that would monitor all of the assets that the agencies own, operate, and maintain.

I think by doing that, you will get more efficiencies, and I think it will dovetail very nicely with the smart city concept. With the smart city concept, I think the platforms that they will be using allows everything to be interconnected, but there needs to be something there, a control center, that monitors all of these assets in real-time to gain more efficiencies with the systems.

Senator FISCHER. As you have this control center that is monitoring in I would assume a more timely and also more accurate manner, how do you see that affecting safety in the future? And also looking at the reliability of our infrastructure, using the example of the Brooklyn Bridge?

Dr. EDELSTEIN. OK. Well, with regard to safety, if it was the Brooklyn Bridge and you had another incident with regard to I–35, the bridge up in Minnesota, hopefully by having the sensors out on the bridge, we could be more proactive in detecting if there is something wrong with the bridge ahead of time so we could make some corrections to it before you have a catastrophe, something like that.

In terms of reliability and other forms of safety, the traffic management centers are already doing that. They are able to detect an incident or a lane closure or an accident a lot faster than the way that we used to do it without the technologies embedded into the systems.

For example, we've been working on a project down in Miami for about the last 10 years operating their control center. When we first started, it took about 15 minutes or so to clear a lane blockage incident. Now it is about half the time. That half the time translates to safety benefits as well as travel time reliability.

In terms of safety benefits, for every minute that we save in a lane-blocking event and clearing that lane that much faster, it translates to nearly 3 percent of probability of a secondary accident happening. So if you take a 15-minute lane-blocking event, take a lane-blocking event and you can clear it 15 minutes faster, you are talking about improving the probability that you won't have a secondary accident by about 40 percent.

In terms of travel time reliability, the formula is, I think for every minute that you save, it translates to 4 minutes of saving. So, again, a 15-minute clearance improvement would translate to about an hour backup delay that you are saving.

So I think it all ties together, whether you are managing assets, or you are managing traffic as well as safety.

Senator FISCHER. Do you see cities and States and also private businesses stepping forward and willing to embrace these new technologies? Is there enthusiasm on their part? Or is it balanced with I guess reality in looking at the cost?

Dr. EDELSTEIN. It is more so the latter. There is definitely enthusiasm. No doubt about it. But many cities are struggling, just paying the day-to-day bills. They have to deal with potholes. They have to deal with physical safety improvements as well as infrastructure improvements that may increase capacity in some of their roadway systems.

Technology is nice. They are looking at that as a long-term solution. But balancing the firefighting issues that they deal with on a day-to-day basis and the budget and the evolution of technology as it comes online, it's pretty tricky.

But I would have to say that most cities and States, they are very enthusiastic about technology innovations. But again, there is just so much money to go around.

Senator FISCHER. Thank you very much.

Senator Booker?

Senator BOOKER. Chair Fischer, Senator Klobuchar has asked if she could go next. She has a committee to return to.

Senator FISCHER. Senator Klobuchar?

STATEMENT OF HON. AMY KLOBUCHAR, U.S. SENATOR FROM MINNESOTA

Senator KLOBUCHAR. Thank you very much. I am the ranking member on this hearing we are having on a bill that we passed last year on sex trafficking, but I want to thank you all for coming. I especially want to thank Mr. Kass who represents here C.H. Robinson, which is headquartered in Eden Prairie, Minnesota, with his 22 years of experience in freight logistics.

As you may know, C.H. Robinson has evolved from a wholesale produce brokerage house to a major third-party logistics provider, is the largest network of motor carrier capacity in North America, had gross revenues of $13.5 billion in 2015, and is one of 17 Fortune 500 companies based in my State. So we are proud of the work that they do and what they can bring to this discussion.

Mr. Kass, could you talk about how you have leveraged the Internet of Things at your company to increase the efficiency of multimodal shipments?

Mr. KASS. Sure. When you think about our company, its focus is on developing technology platforms and services to connect, automate, and optimize supply chains. What the Internet of Things has done is allowed us to create algorithms that quickly and easily select the most optimal mode of transportation.

Many shippers today can't respond in the time, they don't have the resources, they may not even have the expertise, to take a look at what their freight network looks like in real-time and, frankly, shift from a truckload shipment to an intermodal shipment, which poses significant advantages.

The intermodal obviously is going to reduce the carbon footprint. It is going to lower the overall cost. And it is going to take capacity off the road, and I think put it in a safer environment.

Senator KLOBUCHAR. Very good. Thank you very much.

One of the things that we've learned in our state, which I guess we share with all three members who are here today, New Jersey, Nebraska, and Wisconsin, is that you can have all the networks you want for transportation, but if you have snow and the trucks can't move, then we have a problem, or the trains can't go.

I know the Minnesota Department of Transportation has applied for a grant through the U.S. Department of Transportation's Advanced Transportation and Congestion Management Technologies

Deployment Program—that is quite a mouthful—that is used to improve the effectiveness of snowplows.

It is no small thing in our State. We are pretty proud of how quickly we clear out our roads, but technology can always make us better. Let's just say it works a lot better in Minnesota than Washington, D.C.

Dr. Edelstein, how will the new communications opportunities from the Internet of Things improve public safety and the delivery of government services with things like snowplowing?

Dr. EDELSTEIN. Well, if you look at it, let's start with the end-user. The end-user wants their street snowplowed within a certain time-frame or they want to know at least when their street is going to be plowed. By having the Internet of Things, this could provide the communication between the individual and the agency responsible for the plowing, so you open up the communications.

Also, you are opening up the potential to optimize where you have the snowplows, which roads deserve the highest priority. And you can monitor that in real-time, so if you have to do multiple runs of a street because the snow is still coming down, again, you have the potential of using the IoT and big data to optimize the routing of snowplows, assuming that they have automated vehicle location devices on them, or some type of sensors.

Senator KLOBUCHAR. I think that is just a great example because I really am stunned by how long it takes.

My daughter went from the public schools of Minnesota, where she had no snow days for 7 years, and then when she got to the Arlington Public Schools, which are very good, she had 2 weeks off in her first year.

So I do think that there has to be a better way to do that. I understand areas that have more snow are more affected by it.

I guess my last question is just along those same lines, the need to have broadband installation and fast speed broadband to make this work. One of the bills that we have in the MOBILE NOW Act would actually require focus more on dig-one switches to try. When you have highway projects, you try to put the Internet in at the same time to make it more efficient. And obviously many of us on this committee are working on expanding access for broadband in rural areas as well.

Any comments you have about the need to have Wi-Fi to make all of this work?

Dr. EDELSTEIN. That's really outside my expertise, so I'll take a pass on that.

Senator KLOBUCHAR. OK. Can you assume you need Wi-Fi if we are going to have these things on snowplows?

Dr. EDELSTEIN. Yes.

Senator KLOBUCHAR. All right. OK, thank you.

Senator FISCHER. Thank you, Senator Klobuchar.

Senator Booker?

Senator BOOKER. I just want to finish up on the question I was in before about what other countries are doing that is better than the United States, what we can be learning so we can, again, continue to be the global exporter of innovation on the planet Earth.

So, Mr. Davis, you were sort of finishing your answer. I didn't know if you wanted to add any more before I go to Mr. Kass or Dr. Edelstein.

Mr. DAVIS. I'll just add one example. A great technology enabler for the Internet of Things is going to be 5G wireless infrastructure. We see a number of countries moving very quickly there, creating testbeds, creating opportunities to do trials. We'll see it not only in fixed infrastructure that needs to be able to communicate back to a data center or cloud, but even mobile infrastructure.

We see in Germany they are running trials now on the autobahn to learn how to maintain high data rate connectivity when a car is moving very fast down the freeway. We see around the Winter Olympics, Summer Olympics coming up in the future in South Korea and Japan, doing, again, early pilots, early testbeds. I think the more that we can do things to foster——

Senator BOOKER. Why aren't we doing those here?

By the way, with the 5G, some of the innovation is because you have a more predictable, understandable marketplace for innovation and patents and the like over in Europe now than you necessarily do here. Is that some of the reason why?

Mr. DAVIS. I think it is much more about just creating the opportunity. We see these big events like the Winter Olympics or the Summer Olympics. That becomes kind of a focal point for that country to say let's go put a lot of resources in.

Senator BOOKER. So we're not, maybe government is not creating sandboxes where people can——

Mr. DAVIS. I think we want to look for more testbeds. We want to look for opportunities where we can say, hey, let's go all in, let's create a solution to really kind of force the technology to get deployed, for us to understand where we need to do more optimization. I think it is looking for those kinds of opportunities.

Senator BOOKER. OK, thank you.

Jordan, I mean, Mr. Kass, first of all, I want to just echo, because you put in your comments, and it is something that I feel very strongly about, that we have a ridiculously bad tax environment to incentivize companies here. And I see it in biotech with a lot of New Jersey firms inverting now because of the bad environment.

So please don't think that I haven't gotten that point and don't say, basically, hallelujah, amen, and join your chorus of conviction to change that.

But what else are other countries doing besides creating a better tax environment?

Mr. KASS. Firstly, thank you for reading my mind. I appreciate that. That was going to be the way I answered the question.

But secondarily, when I look at our global base of talent and the diversity of it, there is something that is happened here where we are just not developing math students the way that other countries are. And I think that is core to engineering, and it is core to where the Internet of Things is going.

Don't get me wrong, we have talent. But if we are not developing it at the speed and pace that some of these other——

Senator BOOKER. No, we've fallen from number one for graduating engineers, math majors. Now we are out of the top 10.

Other countries are realizing that this new economy is going to necessitate having STEM folks, and America is falling behind.

Mr. KASS. Yes, and then I would add to it the ones that we do, there is a male bias to it, and we need to figure out how to get that neutralized as well. So I would point you in the direction of how we get that fixed.

Senator BOOKER. Great.

Dr. Edelstein, do you have anything to add, especially port efficiency is something that even the Secretary of Transportation and I have talked about, about how in the Northeast people are choosing to use Canadian ports because they are more efficient than ours are. Is there anything that other countries are doing in terms of the Internet of Things for freight logistics that we could be learning from here and catching up on?

Dr. EDELSTEIN. Other countries' freight——

Senator BOOKER. I'll tell you what, Dr. Edelstein, let me move to my last question and try to get it in 10 seconds each. If you had a government dollar, if we were going to be investing, where would you focus your government dollar, Mr. Davis, in terms of getting the biggest return?

Mr. DAVIS. As I said earlier, I think creating these partnerships and these opportunities to really move technology forward, between the private sector, the regulators, and academia.

Senator BOOKER. Jordan?

Mr. KASS. It may surprise everybody, but it would be infrastructure.

Senator BOOKER. Be more specific?

Mr. KASS. Specifically, the road infrastructure. If I painted a picture of the United States, and I showed you the traffic flows around the United States, you would see very clearly on a map where those arteries were unbelievably constricted in major cities around the world.

And there is a trend of urbanization. It is clear. There were 10 megacities, cities over 10 million in population. There were 10 megacities I believe 10 years ago. Now there are 23. People are moving into cities because they need access to products. That trend is clear.

If we don't fix the infrastructure, whatever we do with the Internet of Things is just going to expose the fact that we don't have the infrastructure to move the flow of goods properly.

Senator BOOKER. Tax reform, infrastructure investment. I really like you, Mr. Kass.

[Laughter.]

Senator FISCHER. Thank you.

Senator Blumenthal?

STATEMENT OF HON. RICHARD BLUMENTHAL, U.S. SENATOR FROM CONNECTICUT

Senator BLUMENTHAL. Thank you very much. Thanks for your help and your service.

Because we have a vote, I'm just going to ask you one quick question. Positive Train Control, what can we do to achieve it more quickly and implement it around the country?

Mr. MONJE. Well, I will start. Thank you, Senator. We've been pushing positive train control, and thank you so much for your leadership on this issue.

I think we are very excited at the Department of Transportation that we have $199 million to spend thanks to the FAST Act to help commuter rails get on board. There are still significant challenges across the rail industry to implementing this, including access to spectrum, including equipment issues.

We are doing everything we can. We are working with the FCC. We are working with the class ones. We are working with short lines, with commuter rails. We are doing everything we can to hold their feet to the fire and to make sure we get this technology deployed quickly and safely.

We know that technology would've prevented the crash in Philadelphia. The opportunities for safety are substantial, and we are dedicated to this technology.

Senator BLUMENTHAL. Any other thoughts? How about sensors at rail-grade crossings? These are practical, rail safety measures that will save lives.

Dr. EDELSTEIN. Yes, I think it's an excellent idea. Unfortunately, it takes probably a good mile or so for the train to slow down to get to the point where that person that might be in the railroad crossing would avoid getting hit.

I live in Florida. We just had an incident like that last week, where a family of four was at the railroad crossing. Three of them got out, but one of them got hit by the train.

The communications need to be, obviously, with the driver of the train. To bring it back to the control center wouldn't give you enough time to react.

In urban areas where you have railroad crossing spaced three or four per mile, it becomes a real tricky situation. Now with the Internet of Things, this might be able to be managed a little bit more efficiently than the way we used to do it in the past.

But I think there is a lot of upside potential in addressing these issues in railroad crossings.

Senator BLUMENTHAL. Thank you all.

Thank you.

Senator FISCHER. Thank you, Senator Blumenthal.

I want to thank the witnesses for being here today. I think we had a great hearing, and I appreciate your answers.

The hearing record will remain open for 2 weeks. During this time, Senators are asked to submit any questions for the record. Upon receipt, the witnesses are requested to submit their written answers to the Committee as soon as possible.

With that, the hearing is adjourned.

[Whereupon, at 11:06 a.m., the hearing was adjourned.]

APPENDIX

RESPONSE TO WRITTEN QUESTION SUBMITTED BY HON. RICHARD BLUMENTHAL TO HON. CARLOS MONJE, JR.

Question. In 2008, Congress passed the Rail Safety Improvement Act, which required DOT to issue regulations ensuring that each passenger and freight railroad develop and implement a Risk Reduction Plan "to reduce the numbers and rates of railroad accidents, incidents, injuries, and fatalities." One of the components mandated within the Risk Reduction Plan was a Technology Implementation Plan. The Technology Implementation Plan requires railroads to specify how they will use "current, new or novel technologies" to reduce safety risks.

The 2008 law mandated these regulations governing Risk Reduction Plans—including Technology Implementation Plans—by October 2012. Almost four years since the deadline, there are no final rules ensuring railroads have these plans that incorporate technology into their safety practices.

Mr. Monje, the premise of this hearing is that new technology can enhance safety. Congress mandated that DOT take action to ensure railroads are using technology to save lives. That mandate is outstanding. When will the Department of Transportation carry out the Congressional mandate? When will each railroad be required to have a Technology Implementation Plan?

Answer. The Department's Federal Railroad Administration (FRA) has initiated two rulemakings to implement this mandate: the System Safety Program (SSP) rulemaking for commuter and intercity passenger railroads and the Risk Reduction Program (RRP) rulemaking for Class I railroads and railroads with inadequate safety records. Both rulemakings would require certain railroads to develop and implement an SSP or RRP to improve the safety of their operations. As part of its SSP or RRP, a railroad would be required to set forth a technology implementation plan. To ensure commuter and intercity passenger safety is achieved through an informed rulemaking process, the Railroad Safety Advisory Committee (RSAC) assisted FRA with both rulemakings. The SSP final rule was issued on July 29, 2016 and is expected to be published in the Federal register soon.

An advance notice of proposed rulemaking for the RRP rulemaking was published in the *Federal Register* on December 8, 2010. 75 FR 76345. Two public hearings were held in July 2011. The RRP NPRM was published February 27, 2015 with the comment period ending October 21, 2015. 80 FR 10949 & 80 FR 60591. FRA held a Public Hearing on the RRP NPRM on August 27, 2015. Once again, in an attempt to develop an informed final rule, the RSAC's Risk Reduction Working Group met on September 29, 2015 to review and discuss comments submitted in response to the NPRM. FRA is currently drafting the RRP final rule.